MW01487743

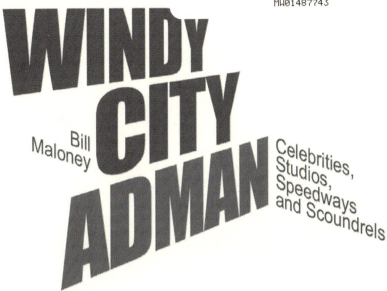

WINDY CITY ADMAN

Bill Maloney

Celebrities,
Studios,
Speedways
and Scoundrels

This is a story about a guy from the Midwest who encountered celebrities and scoundrels on his way to a top career in advertising, auto racing and television.

ISBN: 978-0-9896556-1-3 / ebook   ISBN: 978-0-9896556-0-6 / print version

Ohana Road Publishing   Marina Towers 805   1645 Ala Wai Blvd.   Honolulu, Hi. 96815

*This book is dedicated to my understanding wife
Barbara "Beege" Maloney who fed me while I scribbled.*

*To my daughter, Melanie, who cracked the whip
on us all over the past year.*

*To my son-in-law Vince who encouraged me to
Write this book and to use the "Dragon."*

To my favorite twin gearheads Willy & Sean Maloney

FOREWORD

I first met Bill when he was the host of the "Motorsports International" TV show in Orange County, California on station KDOC. He always had some interesting character, car and news that he brought to life every week.

I specifically remember an episode when he brought out Briggs Cunningham and his 24 Hours of Le Mans race car to bring inside information and insight into the most famous and well-respected endurance race in the world.

As a young man just embarking on my racing career, I thought that I might be able to get some exposure on his TV show and help my sponsors. After one meeting with Bill, I ended up working for him on the TV show as his associate producer! Little did I know at the time how this would help me further my career in auto racing and media.

In his book, you'll find fascinating stories about a self-made ad man/car guy who followed his heart and dreams and really became a mover and shaker in the industry while keeping a humble outlook on life. This is a story about a fellow from the Midwest who encountered celebrities and scoundrels on his way to a top career in advertising, auto racing, television and more.

Throughout this easy read, Bill weaves together and highlights the human aspect of celebrities, the drive you need to succeed and the logistics involved with everything he did coming up through the ranks. It wasn't always easy for him as his time in the military particularly points out.

The stories are fascinating and colorful with a refreshing amount of honesty. In today's world of political correctness, one never knows how someone else really thinks. That's not the case here. Praise and admiration along with a healthy dose of reality checks for certain people are handed out deservedly here.

Bill has rubbed shoulders with some of the best in film, sports and auto racing and influenced many of them along the way. He's been with the who's who in this world and been honored by some of the best. You'll meet some of these people in his book as he gives first-hand accounts of situations they found themselves in.

One thing you won't find in this book is how much Bill has been instrumental in promoting other people to success. Not only did he give me my start in the television world, he also helped me kick-start my radio career again with his "Ohana Road" radio program.

Bill has been a generous guy for many years. I truly marvel at his drive and passion for success and how he's always moving forward.

Congratulations Bill, not only on what you've already done, but what you continue to do on a daily basis. You truly are an inspiration and remember: Keep the tach in the red, and stay ahead!

Enjoy reading this book and be glad that there are people like Bill in this world that set examples for others to follow!

Larry Mason

Larry Mason has won multiple championships in auto racing and has raced everything from go-karts to Indy Lights. He is also a national award-winning journalist and photographer. When he's not at the racetrack, he facilitates new vehicle launch programs for numerous auto manufacturers.

TABLE of CONTENTS

"In the beginning ..."

(The greatest advertising line ever written!)

He was late.

Jonnie was always late but this time it was a big deal. This was The Big Game… at least it was the big game to me… Northwestern vs. Illinois… one of my alma maters vs. the other.

And Jonnie was late.

I had told him that I had the greatest seats in the stadium for Saturday's big football game… one big party.

It was partly my fault he was late. We had met up Friday night and I had introduced him to some of Chicago's more infamous watering holes: Chez Paul, Mr. Kelly's, London House, Little Knight, gave him his football ticket and directions to Dyche Stadium. My boss at the ad agency where I worked, Clint Frank; a Heisman trophy winner from Yale; a very well connected guy. He was on the Board of Trustees for Northwestern so I got 50-yard-line seats for all the games.

It was well into the second quarter and still no Jonnie. Finally, he showed up with a uniformed usher. The usher actually looked like a cop. Jonnie squeezed in beside me. As usual, he was on stage. He grabbed my wrist to make it look like we were tied together. He was getting crazier every minute and telling everyone around us, "I'm a convict at the Joliet State Prison. Tomorrow I go to the electric chair. I'm in for three murders. The Warden agreed to my one last wish: to see my alma mater play football one last time."

Jonnie had everyone convinced I was the Warden and we were handcuffed together. It just got wilder and wilder. Half the fans were watching the football game and half were watching Jonnie's sideshow 23 rows up on the 50-yard-line.

Little did they know. It was still early in his career; he hadn't done any network TV, no commercials. But the people around us on the 50-yard-line were witnessing one of the great, early performances of Jonathan Winters. In a few years, he would be headlining in Vegas, commanding thousands of dollars a week at supper clubs around the nation, keeping Jack Paar in stitches.

But on Saturday November 19, 1955 Jonathan Winters was giving a great free show, one that no one would forget. And he was doing it all with me connected to his wrist.

"This is my Warden. He's a wonderful warden. Thank you, Warden Maloney, for this one last wish."

And with that he kissed me on the cheek.

Maloney and Winters was a great comedy team that afternoon.

There were others over the years. That's because I knew them all, *Jonathan Winters* and *Jackie Cooper, Pat McCormack* and *Paul Williams, Art Linkletter* and *Arte Johnson, Sonja Henie, Mitch Miller,* Hollywood Squares' *Charlie Weaver* and *Wally Cox,* baseball's *Billy Martin* and more race car drivers than you could shake a stick shift at. Had drinks with most of them. Had multiple drinks with more than a few. Even had to duck a punch from *Billy Martin*!

It was all part of my job.

I was an Ad Man.

Not a Mad Man. Those were the guys in New York, so called because many of their advertising agencies were located on Madison Avenue.

I was an Ad Man, a **Windy City Ad Man**, *based in Chicago, in the early days of television, when Chicago and New York were vying for supremacy in the advertising game.*

We always said they had style but we had content.

And we had it in spades.

Marketing trade magazine writers and financial columnists once loved to yak about the "Chicago school of advertising" vs. the "New York school of advertising." The big agencies in New York like Doyle Dane Bernbach and Ogilvy & Mather created some great stuff: "The Man in the Hathaway Shirt;" "VW, Think Small." But the guys in Chicago, Tatham Laird, Campbell Ewald, Foote Cone and Belding and Leo Burnett were doing outstanding stuff too, creating the Marlboro Man, Ronald McDonald, the Jolly Green Giant and the Pillsbury Doughboy.

Legendary Creative Director and agency owner Leo Burnett was a six-day-a-week hard working visionary ad guy. He often said that as far as awards were concerned, he'd rather have great product rather than great ads. Leo was a Chicago business icon having started his ad agency in 1935. When I met him on a Northwestern commuter train in 1954, his shop was billing $22 million. He was part of the "creative revolution" in Chicago advertising style as agencies took bolder approaches re-marketing a variety of products. In the ad game. *Time Magazine* named him one of the 100 most influential people of the 20th century in America.

I put in over 50 years of fun and frolic in the volatile world of advertising, marketing and television production, working for many major clients: Hallmark, Butterfinger, Kleenex, General Motors, Chrysler, Canadian Club, Reynolds Metals, all the while getting involved intensely with sports car racing, producing my own automotive TV shows, writing for car magazines and major newspapers plus trying to maintain a family… *er,* families.

I ran around with entertainers and creators. I once had an office next to the guy who wrote, *"You'll wonder where the yellow went when you brush your teeth with Pepsodent,"* down the hall from the guy who wrote the Dodge Charger line, *"You in a heap a trouble boy,"* and in the same office with the guy who wrote *"Porsche Spoken Here."* Oh wait, that was **me** that wrote that last one!

While my fraternity brothers from the University of Illinois and Northwestern were toiling away in sales training programs at such less-than-exciting Forbes 500 firms as National Cash Register, Proctor & Gamble and Allstate Insurance, I was boozing down New York's Broadway, getting looped on Chicago's Loop, escorting clients into Studio 8-H at 30 Rock, tippling at Toots Shor's and hanging with show biz dudes and dudettes on the Sunset Strip.

Jeez, it was frantic but it was fun!

CHAPTER ONE

From the Jazz Age to World War II... what a hell of a ride ...
ad world here I come!

"Grump" and me... cars... the Ice Cream Mountains and boxing

I was born in the Jazz Age and grew up in the Depression, a
dichotomy that must have shaped my personality. I grew up chasing
fun and money!

I think I got my adventurous side from my Grandfather McCarron.
We called him "Grump," even though he was the furthest thing
from an old grump.

William "Grump" McCarron was a tremendous influence on me. I was
more McCarron (cars and creativity) than I was Maloney (studious).
I was almost a clone of "Grump." He was an entrepreneur and had
been involved for years with cars and trucks. He would spend hours
showing me plans and blueprints he prepared for a unique truck
that featured four-wheel steering.

In 1936, he invented a police car ambulance that was used by the
Chicago Police Department; it was a squad car with the back seat
and trunk customized to carry injured people similar to a mini
ambulance. He actually built a McCarron truck and it sold fairly well.

It was "Grump" who got me interested in cars – all aspects of cars.
He owned two Ford dealerships in Chicago and I spent a great deal
of time puttering around the showrooms and service areas, getting
grease under my fingernails as well as learning from the salesmen
how to jimmy the candy bar machines for goodies. Fun and money!

He was colorful, full of stories and always tinkering. He would visit all
his grandchildren and spin tales about taking us all to the "Ice Cream
Mountains," "Root Beer River," "Candy Canyons," and we believed
him. We pestered our parents to let us go to those wonderful places.

Much to the chagrin of my parents he took us to the Friday Night
Fights in Cicero, the mob suburb of Chicago; bloody amateur
boxing matches.

I got my practical side from my dad, Joseph Maloney, who studied his way out of Chicago's melting pot neighborhood to become a CPA and a lawyer. He was an avid sports fan and was Papa Bear George Halas's first CPA for the Chicago Bears' NFL franchise. Money was tight at the fledgling Bear's lair in the late 1920's so Halas paid him partly in season tickets. We had six of the best box seats for 50 years. At an early age, I began attending Bears games at Wrigley Field and became a Bears fan. All of us in our family loved sports and rotated our Bears tickets among all seven of us including mom, Marie.

I was always the little guy in school but at the Campion Military Academy (high school) in Prairie Du Chien, Wisconsin; the Jesuits made certain you participated in all sorts of sports. The campus had four football fields, three gymnasiums, hockey rinks and baseball diamonds. No matter what your size or weight there was a team for you to join. I played guard in basketball; first base in baseball; center in hockey; left end on the lightweight football team with QB Jack Rockne, son of legendary Notre Dame Coach, Knute Rockne.

Later at Fenwick High School in Oak Park, Illinois, I won the prestigious Silver Gloves Boxing Championship (112 lbs.) and two speed skating titles.

City Silver Gloves Boxing Champion, Fenwick High School in Oak Park, Illinois 1944.
I was small but powerful, poised for a parallel career as a race car driver
where there are "no limits."

Grump taught me how to drive in his 1942 Nash and wanted me to be his driver when he headed for his annual vacation in Fort Lauderdale. My parents said no. High school got in the way.

At the age of 76, we got word that he had pulled off the road somewhere in Georgia and had a heart attack and died. Bye Grump. What a colorful guy who left a lasting influence on me.

*Though mom said "**NO**" to my first auto race, I was Don "Crash" Carter at Soldier Field*

I was getting car happy as I had frittered a lot of after school time hanging out with a bunch of Oak Park hot rodders. While my proper Catholic high school classmates were practicing golf and playing cards, I was pulling old cars apart in local junkyards and drag racing. I even built a 1937 chopped and channeled Ford hot rod that I took to the Soldier Field Hot Rod Races in Chicago intending to race it. The competition turned out to be a 15 car contingent of professional Hot Rod racers from California who learned about big race pur$e$ and came to Chicago to clean up on us amateurs. Then my mother got wind of my plans. She called the track and said she would close it if they allowed underage me to race. I was seventeen… the entry blank said you must be 21 years of age.

Years later, I met Andy Granatelli, a huge name in auto racing and CEO of the STP motor Oil additive company and promoter of the Hurricane Hot Rod Association races with a spectator turnout of 40,000 on hand. My crew and I had worked long hours to get the hot rod ready to race and we had already paid the $25 entry fee. *I was ready to race.* So I changed my name on the entry form to Don "Crash" Carter and went out to qualify my car. Three laps into my run on the quarter mile track I smacked the wall, broke an axle and that was the end of my race day. And my mom was none the wiser.

A sidebar on Soldier Field: Years before my fiasco, Soldier Field was known for hosting the largest attendance, 123,000, at any collegiate sporting event, November 26, 1927, Notre Dame vs. University of Southern California. In Chicago, that meant the Catholics vs. the West Coast Protestants.

And then the war came. I was only 14 when World War II broke out, and I was itching to get into the action. But at my height and my weight there was no way I could fool a recruiter into thinking I was 18. And there was no way my dad would sign for me to get in early. He wanted me in college.

Not knowing what was ahead after high school graduation from Fenwick, 1944.

I meet my first "scoundrel"… He bought Der Fuhrer's Mercedes

One of my "acquaintances" at the time was Tommy Barrett, *the* Barrett of Barrett-Jackson Classic Auto Auction fame. He and I went to grammar school together and later ran around when I took summer school at Oak Park High, Ernest Hemingway's school in Oak Park, Illinois.

Tom was a complete car nut. While most of us were studying our algebra lessons, waiting for the war to end, Tom was peddling used cars… in high school! One of his nefarious tricks was to spot a Gold Star in the window of a local home, go to the door and offer the widow or mother of the fallen serviceman his condolences and then say, "Want to sell his Buick?" Tasteless. But it worked and he made a lot of money selling those cars.

When he was about 19, Tom bought Adolf Hitler's Mercedes Benz Command car that had been spirited back to the U.S. by an enterprising Army officer with connections. He took it around to state fairs throughout the Midwest charging a buck for people to check out the huge Panzer Phaeton adorned with swastikas. This was a hot item as World War II just ended and anything connected to Hitler found a huge audience.

Tom went on to become Barrett-Jackson Classic Car Auctions, and he made millions. Tom was the guy who invented classic car collecting and auctions. I knew he made millions because years later at the Pebble Beach Concourse in Monterey he told me that he was taking his Rolls-Royce limousine on the QE2 to Europe.

That's heavy.

The U.S. Navy sends me to hell… Hawthorne, Nevada

My best friend all through high school was next-door neighbor John McKittrick. We walked to Fenwick High School classes every day, went out on dates, played sports and when we turned 18 and the war was still going on, enlisted in the U.S. Navy together. We were both sent to Great Lakes Naval Training Center north of Chicago for our boot camp and were both shipped out at the same time; John to an APA/troop ship in San Francisco and me to an ammo dump in the middle of Nevada. What bum luck for me.

WHICH ONE IS BILL

Anchors Aweigh! Little did we know we were headed for the Nevada desert, not the Pacific.

After boot camp, the Navy asked where I wanted to serve and I said, "submarines, destroyers or someplace exotic." True to form, the Navy never even considered my request so I was sent to Hawthorne, Nevada. It was a frigid 30 degrees in the morning and a sizzling 100 plus at noon. Ammo dump… and aptly named… a dump… three hours southeast of Reno and five hours northwest of Las Vegas.

We were messing with all sorts of ammunition and found a lot of the stuff dated to World War I, 1917. We even found cases of shells from a munitions plant in Pennsylvania where a female "bomb maker" would leave notes for the GI's. "Hi I'm Betty… Call me at…" Of course we'd laugh as we visualized what Betty looked like 26 years later when we were unpacking her bombs.

Hawthorne was pretty grim. It had only four thousand local residents so the only recreation for 18 year-old sailors was a few saloons with gambling. A guy could spend or blow his entire $35 Navy month's pay in one night in Hawthorne… and we usually did.

Base security was handled by the U.S. Marines. They were the sailors' mortal enemies as they performed Shore Patrol Police duty and hindered our fun and frolic. SP's were the service cops and we tried to avoid them when partying. Because of their gaudy blue, red and grey uniforms, we called them *seagoing bellhops*. They hated that title.

The Marines (who we also called Gyrenes) dress uniforms also included a huge metal belt buckle that was a perfect weapon in a fight. Rip it off your pants, wrap it around your fist and you almost had brass knuckles. Some more obstreperous sailors countered this by sewing 20mm anti-aircraft shells into the back of their neckerchiefs which acted like a bolero in a skirmish with the Shore Patrols or any other Marines who attempted to spoil our fun.

At Hawthorne, I hung with my Chicago gang: Norm Perino, South Chicago; Ken McDonald, Evergreen Park; Ray Touhy (we called him Roger Touhy after the South Side Chicago gangster) from Cottage Grove; Tom Mulcahy, Evanston. And there was Big Ernie Johnson from Maywood who decided he would be my protector. He was six feet tall and 220 pounds. He liked to harden his fists by punching trees. We all were pretty certain Big Ernie wasn't playing with a full deck. But he was nice to have around.

The highpoint of my seven month stint at Hawthorne Naval Ammo Dump was flying out in a Grumman Avenger to Alameda, California to join the crew of the U.S.S. Barton, DD722, a Sumner class 2200-ton Destroyer equipped with six 5"x 38 sea rifles, 12 – 40mm anti-aircraft guns (my battle station), 11 – 20mm guns, six torpedo tubes and six depth charge racks.

It had a top speed of 35 knots and was called a "tin can" for good reason. I was sick for three days, first time out to sea. The cooks thought they would rub it in as we new guys searched for our sea legs and they served us greasy pork chops and ice cream... and they laughed at our misery.

"Hey, sailor... you got any money?" asked the hooker.

The low point of my "time served" at Hawthorne was my ill-advised, ill-fated hitchhiking junket 300 miles to San Francisco to meet my pal McKittrick.

We each had a weekend liberty pass and decided to meet at a USO in downtown San Francisco on a Saturday noon. Heck... 300 miles at 60 MPH should take about seven or eight hours. It took 24 hours.

I was too naïve to realize that back then motorists did not pick up servicemen. In fact, I stood in one spot on a desolate Nevada highway for eight hours attempting to flag a ride. Finally a trucker picked me up and then more trouble. My wallet with ID and money was in a shallow pocket on my hip in my dress blues and as I curled up in the passenger seat of the semi, it must have fallen out (or was stolen) and I arrived in San Francisco to meet John, 10 hours late with no money and no ID. **Grim.**

We had a couple beers... caught up on old and new times and I was off to the highway to get back to Hawthorne by 8:00 a.m. Monday. Again, I stood four hours freezing by the side of the road, barely visible in the dark, clad in my Navy blues and black pea coat which I took off to in an effort to encourage a feeling of mercy from motorists as I stood in the snow swept darkness freezing to death.

Then a miracle happened. Two gals in a late model Buick stopped and said hop in. First thing they said was, "Hey Sailor... You got any money?"

I told them my sad story and they were peeved. No dough. We drove. Me in the backseat freezing and with hundreds of miles left to go to Hawthorne. They were bound for Reno. They chatted and I couldn't believe the gross language. My Navy pals weren't even this down and dirty. These were two tough chicks and there's me, seven months out of a Dominican high school.

It turned out they were two hookers and had stolen the car from one of their johns. They had very little money and were almost out of gas.

We found a gas station open at 4:00 a.m. and the two babes sold the radio in the Buick to the station guy for a tank of gas. Then, sensing there may be a checkpoint at the California - Nevada state line, they gave me a screwdriver, drove down a side street and told me to steal a license plate off a parked car. I did. It was desperation.

We took off and I held my breath for three more hours until they dropped me off at the Hawthorne guard gate. As much as I disliked the place I could not have been happier to be back in civilization.

I was a minor league hero to my gang; after all, I had spent an entire night with two Las Vegas hookers.

>*"You want sea duty, Seaman Maloney?"*
>*Be careful what you wish for!*

In my letters home, I kept moaning to my mother and father about Hawthorne. I continued to complain that I didn't join the Navy to be stuck in an ammo dump. I wanted to see the world...
not sit on a rock.

Actually, I joined the Navy in 1944 to keep from being drafted into the U.S. Army. The term of my enlistment was for the *duration and six,* meaning from the time war is officially declared over, I had another six months in the Navy and then I'd be discharged.

My father attended St. Ignatius High School with Chicagoan Daniel V. Gallery. He forwarded my letters to Gallery, now a U.S. Navy Captain, at his base in Alameda, California aboard the aircraft carrier U.S. S. Rendova, CVE 114 (Carrier Vessel Escort), a ship with a crew of 1,000 and 34 Chance Vaught Corsair and Grumman Avenger fighter planes.

Gallery had his aide, Lt. David Ward, write a letter to me asking what I had in mind. I replied that I just wanted sea duty. The war was winding down and I thought a destroyer would be great duty.

It would be fast and forbidding.

"You sure you want sea duty, Seaman Maloney?" World War II aboard the U.S.S. Barton in the Pacific.

I knew Navy captains really ruled their turf. They were kings of all they surveyed, but I wasn't prepared for what was about to unfold with my desire for sea duty.

One mild and boring Hawthorne afternoon as I was wheeling my jeep around the ammo complex, I heard an unfamiliar airplane engine. My buddies heard it too and knew it was not the lumbering Douglas DC-3's that came to our base once a month with our payroll. It was also the wrong time for the money plane. This bird was an aircraft-based Navy Torpedo plane and it was 320 miles from the Pacific Ocean.

Somehow I knew it was for me and that I was about to embark on a new adventure. As a dozen loudspeakers blared, *"Maloney, Seaman First Class up to the quarterdeck office on the double… bring your packed sea bag."*

Gulp.

Within an hour I was buckled into the rear gunner's turret of the warplane. Terrified. What if I hit the wrong switch and the turret started to rotate and I didn't rotate? Maybe the Plexiglas bubble turns but my seat doesn't? Twisted to death... what a way to die. At 25,000 feet, encased in a glass bubble, it was hot.

The pilot, Dave Ward, Captain Gallery's aide, had a girlfriend in Reno so we spent the night there; he with the girlfriend and me in a $5 a night flop house. I wondered what this little aerial junket was costing the taxpayers.

When we got to Alameda Naval Air Station, I had the choice of becoming part of the crew on Captain Gallery's Aircraft Carrier (which looked as if it was going to be parked in Alameda for a long time) or head out to sea on some kind of ship. I asked for a "tin can." And here is why: it was widely known throughout the Navy that if you were related to or closely acquainted with a Navy V.I.P you were considered to have P.I. (Personal/Public Influence). It even went into your Navy Jacket (file). It was fine for working with officers but enlisted men could treat you as some sort of pariah; i.e. teacher's pet. Not fun. I had clearly received preferential treatment.

Two days later, I'm told to pack up and head for the small boat dock. With my sea bag, I jumped into a Navy Chris Craft speedboat and we took off for the broad Pacific Ocean chasing the "tin can" five miles as it was steaming out to sea. Unreal. The ship was running at about 10 knots as we pulled up to its fantail. I threw my 20-pound sea bag onto the deck and two sailors hoisted me aboard.

Well... I wanted sea duty... and I got it.

I had no papers, no specific duties, was not expected and didn't even have a bunk. The next couple of "orientation weeks" were interesting. Nobody on the ship knew who I was, what my rank was, where I belonged, where I came from and I was an unknown crewmember as my papers were still back in Alameda. It took a week for the ship's office to receive word that, yes, I was a new crewman.

"Put him to work."

Two weeks later the war ended... just as I was getting my sea legs.

"I'm done with cars," I said, as I headed to college.
Little did I know!

After my Navy discharge, I floundered around with my hot rod pals, Knut, Benny, Dobber and Louie. We built motors and drank beer.

My father, who not only was a CPA but also had a law degree, was not happy about this situation and was after me to go to college. He had a young man visit us who wanted me to join his Catholic fraternity, Phi Kappa Theta. My dad had attended college at Loyola University but he thought a state college might be easier to get into with my G.I. Bill benefit.

I thought about it and finally it came to a head one day, as I was lying on the ground at our gas station/club house in Oak Park trying like mad to get a frozen four-cylinder race motor to turn over. I had been at it for several days using a variety of lubricants, tools, sledge hammers and busting my chops with no success.

As I lay in a pool of sweat on a beautiful sunny spring day, a shiny Ford convertible with the top down, two girls in it and a University of Illinois pennant flying, drove by. I was hooked. I knew there had to be something better than this. Hot rodding suddenly sucked and I was through with it.

I got out from under the car, collected my tools, went into the gas station where my troops were hanging out and said, "Guys I'm through with cars. First 10 bucks takes my car."

Slam bam came the sawbucks. I collected one and walked out. I never played with cars again for 15 years.

"Don't ever consider a career in accounting, Mr. Maloney"

I packed up and headed to Springfield Junior College in Springfield, Illinois to get prepped for U of I. One of my classes at Springfield Junior College was accounting, and I was the worst student in the class. Really bad, even though my father was a partner in the prestigious Peat Marwick & Mitchell, one of the largest CPA firms in the world.

The semester exams came around, and I was lost but I attempted to take the finals.

The instructor, Mr. Johnson took me aside and said, "Mr. Maloney, don't ever, ever think about a career in accounting. You have to be just about the worst student I've ever had. However I'm going to give you a passing grade to get you out of here because your father, Joe, was my instructor at Loyola and I thought he was the very best. I owe him. Go away!"

Off to U of I finally… and lots of new gigs

Even though the accounting class was a disaster, I had enough credits plus my G.I. Bill benefits to immediately enroll at the University of Illinois, Champaign-Urbana. They had an option for World War II veterans called, DSSWV, Division of Special Services for War Veterans. It meant the veteran could take any course he or she wanted to take (P.E., basket weaving, history of naval warfare or even a pilot's license which I did) as long as the credits added up.

I knew from my journalism and advertising classes at Illinois that I wanted to get involved with something that had to do with television and automobiles. If I did any serious studying it was hours in the library learning about the new medium called television.

I also did a weekly radio acting gig on the U of I station, **WILL**, and wrote sports features for the campus newspaper, *The Daily Illini*. At the same time, Hugh Hefner was doing cartoons for the paper.

And the Chicago mobster said, "They last guy who tried the parlay card game had a real bad accident…"

My other part time job at U of I was the football parlay card concession, and it thrived.

My pal, fellow student and World War II ex-Army Ranger, Bill Ryan, was a real live professional Chicago gambler who mostly played the horses. We bonded and figured the U of I student body was ready for the football parlay card racket.

As a war veteran, I was allowed to have a car on campus so each Monday when the "Chicago syndicate" sent our 500 football parlay cards to us ($100) via Illinois Central train to Urbana, I'd pick them up and distribute them to my "agents" in 16 fraternities and 12 sororities. Bill did the same with students living in dorms.

The students would make their bets and I'd meet the agent Saturday morning at Kam's beer joint on campus to collect the cards and the money… mostly dollar wagers. Bill and I did quite well with the football cards… and yes; it was a bit on the chancy side. Sunday night when all the college and professional scores were finalized we'd get together and go through the cards for payoffs.

I remember one Saturday I'm meeting all my agents at Kam's. I'm with a naïve young sorority gal from Effingham, Illinois and we have a pile of cash on the table… a huge pile.

And she says "Wow, gee willikers… I've never been with a real live gangster before!" Ding bat.

At 21 years old I had to have my tonsils out. Not a good age for this. I bled for five days and it was looking bad. Couldn't stop bleeding. Finally did. Back to U of I for a sorority dance. Here's what I looked like with Gloria "The Glo Girl" Gables from Lake Forest, Illinois.

That's when I started dressing like actor Richard Widmark who was then starring as the treacherous hoodlum Tommy Udo. He pushed an old lady in a wheelchair down a flight of stairs in the flick "Kiss Of Death" wearing his black shirt, yellow tie and white sport coat. How many people knew he was originally a drama teacher at Lake Forest College near Chicago?

With a "bettors market" of 17,000 students, the word got out to *The Mob* who horned into our campus racket. They sent one of their "boys" to pay me a visit at the Sigma Nu Fraternity House. The hood showed up when I was out of town and scared the crap out of one of the pledges.

The hood was right out of Damon Runyon… fedora, overcoat, collar up, gruff voice saying he was looking for the guy who was running the parlay cards business.

When told I was not in the house he returned the following week. Same Runyon-esque get-up, but this time we were stuck meeting with him. He "offered" to take Ryan and me into their organization so we'd have their financial security and protection "for a cut of the action."

"What would happen if some fraternity guy got lucky and put up $10 and got ten correct scores?" he asked. "Can you cover $1,000?"

I declined his offer and said we were thinking of taking our "action" down the road to Danville, an infamous "loose" town of gambling and prostitution.

The hood said, "That could be a mistake. The last guy who tried it had an accident… real bad accident." A threat?

Yep.

Walter Winchell shuts us down

Big dude national columnist Walter Winchell put a note in one of his columns about the "football parlay card racket at University of Illinois," and we were out of business. It seems he somehow got wind of our "campus racket" and put a squib in his New York Daily Mirror column and mentioned it on his ABC Network radio gossip show.

A U of I Board of Regents member heard it, and the school came down on Ryan and me. *Finito.* And probably none too soon.

After Walter Winchell effectively closed down our University of Illinois football parlay card racket, Bill Ryan and I looked around for another source of after-hours revenue.

More antics at U of I… Maloni and Ryoni Pizza

A fraternity brother, Ed Mite (real name Mitelski, a hard-working Chicago Polish guy who changed his name) decided after graduation not to leave Champaign-Urbana with its 40,000 well-heeled students (also known as "sales prospects") so he opened a home delivery dry cleaning establishment. He found a good-sized bakery that had gone under, leased the building and started his dry-cleaning adventure. He obviously didn't need the huge ovens but did need the large space to hang racks of dry cleaning. He asked me to help him with this nice fairly new modern facility. In fact, I named his business "Prom-Mite Cleaners."

Bill Ryan spent two years in an Italian prison camp and he claimed to know everything there was to know about making pizza. We both knew that little neighborhood pizza parlors were sprouting up all over Chicago and the pizza business was really getting hot. Why not go into the pizza business? We had Ed Mite's beautiful off-campus bakery with its huge rotisserie ovens, long tables for prep and cutting at our disposal. Ed's cleaning business was in another part of the building and he had no use for the ovens.

We got serious about pizza. "*Pizza…* while you're studying each night, delivered to your door" was the headline in the colorful flyers we handed out to all the campus Greek houses and independent dorms.

Lasting friendships with the brothers of Sigma Nu fraternity, University of Illinois. I'm first row, second from end on the right.

I had my parlay card "agents" in 16 fraternities and 12 sororities and several dorms that told us that a piping hot pizza delivered to studying students would be the hot ticket. My agents were excited. As a veteran, I had a new car for delivery chores. And that was a big plus. We also found an old panel truck that we stuffed with mattresses to retain the pizza warmth.

So, we had an up-to-date bakery, Bill Ryan's cooking expertise, 28 Greek houses ready for product, a delivery car and lots of energy to devote to this new scheme. But there was one problem: Maloney and Ryan did not sound Italian enough or Pizza-ish. So we named our fledgling enterprise:

Maloni and Ryoni Hot Pizza.

As we were starting to think about menus, buying ingredients, advertising to the fraternities and the kind of new cars we'd buy with our first hundred grand profits, it became time to actually make a pizza.

Ryan said he knew all about the ingredients and the secret one was fennel seed. We turned Bill loose in our frat house kitchen to turn out the initial signature Maloni and Ryoni pizza pie.

To say it was crummy, crappy and inedible would be kind. It was a disaster. Ryan did not know how to make pizza. The stuff actually made us sick. Yuk. Finito again.

That was the end of Maloni and Ryoni Hot Pizza.

As a P.S. to our pizza career… Three years later, Notre Dame Alum Tom Monahan got into the pizza racket. He created Domino's, which is now in every state with stores in 61 countries.

He made so much money he bought the Detroit Tigers baseball team, collected Dusenberg classic cars and was big donor to Catholic charities.

I wrote Monahan, a fellow motor head, and told him how we almost scooped him at U of I but we didn't know jack about cooking pizza. He wrote me a pleasant letter saying he had a lot of luck and it turned out just great… Good luck to us.

*Arte Johnson
re-wrote my skit*

I knew Arte Johnson at U of I. Years later, he was a comic on the wildly successful TV Show, "Laugh-In." Arte was in the Jewish fraternity Sigma Alpha Mu ("the Sammy's") and their house was next to my fraternity's, Sigma Nu. He was always funny, and like Jonathan Winters, he was always "on."

One of the last things I was involved with before I left U of I in 1950 was writing a vaudeville skit for Sigma Nu. This was for the annual Illinois all-fraternity variety show and I called my skit "Breadline." Set in the Depression, it featured dozens of crazy and talented people on the "Breadline." I gave my frat brothers the script and hightailed it to the Windy City. I later learned that Arte had taken my script and really chopped it up. I was really chagrined. How dare he?

Later when he became a TV star, I didn't feel so bad. In fact I felt pretty good. Arte Johnson, a real pro, thought enough of my work to rewrite it!

Years later, I ran into him in a Greenwich Village bar and it was old home week… talked well into the wee hours of the morning.

CHAPTER TWO

How I Got to the Chicago School of Advertising

I loved the babes in the sorority houses, I partied hearty with the guys in my frat but I didn't like the 20-page term papers or the visits from Cicero mobsters. So, in 1950 I left the University of Illinois, a few hours shy of a B.A. I felt like I had a B.S. and that was enough. I was ready to get on with my life.

I made a brief stop at Northwestern University for a couple of journalism courses and to again use the veteran's DSSWV program.

Finally... I was ready for the ad business. Was it ready for me?

The Chicago school vs. The New York School

Marketing trade magazine writers and financial columnists once loved to yak about the "Chicago school of advertising" vs. the "New York school of advertising." The big agencies in New York like Doyle Dane Bernbach and Ogilvy & Mather created some great stuff; "The Man in the Hathaway Shirt," "VW, Think Small." In Chicago, Tatham Laird, Campbell Ewald, Foote Cone and Belding were doing good work as was Leo Burnett Agency's creation of The Marlboro Man, the McDonald's campaigns plus The Jolly Green Giant and The Pillsbury Doughboy programs.

Some said the New York school had *style*. The Chicago school's hallmark was *content*.

Moving into the fast-paced ad world... learning the ropes

The Russell M. Seeds Advertising Agency occupied the top two floors of the Palmolive Building next to the Drake Hotel on Michigan Avenue bordered by Lake Shore Drive in Chicago. The building would later become the Playboy Building. It was a very prestigious address with a penthouse and 37 floors. At the apex of Windy City windiness, we could actually watch the building sway as the pictures on the wall stood still and the building moved.

This was my first ad agency job. I had worked here as an office boy during summer college breaks. Now I had a "step-up" job, though a very humdrum job in the research department. This soon changed and I became a traffic manager, which meant I had to convince copywriters to meet their closing date deadlines before they could go to their three-martini lunch. Now, for the first time, I had my own office, and a real title: Production Control Manager.

After a year, I was offered a job as a radio/ TV producer at the number two ad agency in Chicago: Foote Cone and Belding. I couldn't turn it down. I got a cool office in "producers row," an interesting title, and responsibility for some blue-chip accounts including Hallmark, Kleenex and Frigidaire.

Next to my office was my pal and super wordsmith, Don Williams, who created the award-winning ad campaign, "You'll wonder where the yellow went when you brush your teeth with Pepsodent." He got a heck of a raise after he penned that!

Somehow over the years I had developed a "multi-tasking trait." This was long before Microsoft and Apple were promising the ability to "multi-task." In every job I had, I would need more "stuff" to keep me occupied. I needed more challenges other than holding down just one job. It started at U of I with my side gig parlay card business all while I was going to class, playing intramural sports, working at the radio station work and chasing sorority girls.

At the Russell M. Seeds Agency, I had created two retail research panels, one of drugstores and the other of jewelers; 50 of them in six Midwestern states where we could preflight ad promotions for clients such as Schaeffer Pen, Raleigh Cigarettes and Elgin watches before a campaign kick-off.

Learning from Clinton E. Frank, Heisman winner…
wildly successful start-up ad agency

Clint Frank was a genuine Chicago hero, a Yale graduate, 1936, an All-American halfback and the third Heisman Trophy winner. In 1954, he was starting his new advertising agency in Chicago. He'd taken the Reynolds Metals ad account away from the Russell Seeds Agency and with it, the account supervisor Wade Grinstead, who later would become my mentor.

Clinton E. Frank, CEO of Cinton E. Frank Advertising was not only a brilliant adman but was also the third Heisman Trophy Winner, Yale, 1937.

Clint and Wade needed an account executive/TV producer to work on Reynolds. Wade said he wanted me for the job after he'd heard, via the Chicago ad grapevine, of my various successes and the U-505 German Submarine project. Clint told Wade to "find a way to hire Bill."

After a long dinner at the very exclusive Yale Club where every big shot in the club came to Clint's table, he pitched and I appeared hooked.

It was a tough decision. Did I go with a new ad agency with $10 million in advertising billing versus an established, prestigious Four A's $100 million shop?

I went with Clint; a risk that I was very happy with as now I was a *real* ad executive instead of just another one of FC & B's 300 employees. The salary was $12 grand per year. Wow!

I had vowed to make a $10 grand salary before I was 30 years old.

Done!

Clint was Chicago society… family money… General James Doolittle's aide-de-camp… lived in the high-rent section of Wilmette (North Shore) in a gorgeous home with an unbelievable basement party room highlighted by the glass-encased Heisman Trophy!

Great products with lots of variety

A benefit derived from working at a mid-sized ad agency such as Clinton E. Frank, Inc. was the opportunity to be involved with the marketing programs variety of products. In my case, I was the account executive for such diverse products as Reynolds Wrap, Reynolds Hardware, Reynolds Industrial Markets, Curtiss Candy, Wurlitzer Pianos & Organs and the Chicago Chevrolet dealers. These were all very active and demanding accounts and kept everyone hopping.

After five years in the bowels of the Chicago's Merchandise Mart, Clinton E. Frank took over the two-story penthouse offices of the Mart, then the world's largest office building.

Clint's dynamic leadership was making our company a real force in the Chicago ad game. We added Conoco Oil, Toni, Quaker Oats, and we opened offices in New York and Los Angeles.

The Big Time!… Reynolds Metals… "Mr. Peepers"… Cliff Arquette and Charlie Weaver… on NBC live prime time… Wow!

This was a far cry from the ammunition dump hell in Hawthorne, Nevada! Our prize client was Reynolds Metals and they jealously guarded their prestigious NBC Sunday 7:00 p.m. time slot, home to their Peabody award winning sitcom, "Mr. Peepers." When "Mr. Peepers" went off for a summer hiatus, Reynolds judiciously secured the sought-after time period by sponsoring a couple of 13-week, low-budget, low-audience turkeys.

One show was called "Circus Boy," a half-hour based on circus life starring a young boy who works in a travelling circus. One of the stars was likeable character actor, Noah Berry Jr., a guy who introduced me to a New Orleans cocktail called "Sazarak" at the Pump Room in Chicago. I still have that licorice taste in my mouth.

The other 13-week sitcom was called "Do It Yourself," and it featured Cliff Arquette as Charlie Weaver and his woodworking sidekick, the versatile veteran actor Dave Willock. While people remember Weaver from his hilarious appearances on TV variety shows, especially the Jack Parr program, few people realize Dave made over 48 feature movies. He was always some sort of second banana. He was everywhere.

CHARLIE WEAVER

Cliff Arquette, me and Dave Willock kidding around before a live 1955 NBC show, "Do It Yourself." Cliff was widely known as "Charlie Weaver." I was Reynolds Metals Account Executive.

The new summer replacement, the "Do It Yourself" show centered around a couple of bumbling guys and their family travails. They were always building something in their garage workshop. Cue: snore. Cliff, of course, did everything wrong and likeable Dave would straighten him out. The fact that Reynolds Metals made 40 variations of do-it-yourself aluminum products kind of made this show almost an infomercial, long before that term had been coined.

And it was a sitcom; therefore, *Tim Allen did not have the first "Home Improvement" show!*

Running with the big boys… and girls

If I were an astronaut, the G-forces would have killed me.

Things were moving quickly.

Before the series kicked off, I had an idea as to how we could get a ton of national publicity for "Do It Yourself," possibly even cover stories from a variety of men's magazines such as *Family Handyman, Popular Mechanics, Popular Science, Argosy*, and other "do-it-yourself" men's publications.

Simple: we'd plug the publication in our network television show, and in return, they would give us editorial coverage.

From my Chicago office, I got on the phone and made appointments with seven magazines in New York City. When I got there, I started the New York workday with a 9:00 a.m. appointment and met with another publication every two hours.

I promised each publication that their magazine would be shown on NBC's "Do-it-Yourself," great network television exposure for them, with millions of viewers watching, *if* they ran a story about our TV show. And they did. And we obviously cooperated by plugging the publication in our shows. This clearly hyped our TV show viewership.

But in executing my plan, I got myself in the cross hairs of a high-powered New York public relations woman named Ursula Halloran, who was employed by Reynolds to do exactly what I just accomplished with one day of shoe leather.

Ursula, my age, President of Ursula Halloran Associates, with an office on Fifth Avenue, was a real super power in the television PR business. She had been Miss Pittsburgh. In later years, Bob Hope discovered her and cast her in his "My Favorite Brunette" movie.

She learned the business working for Rogers and Cowan in Hollywood, the first major PR firm for movie and TV celebrities, and then she started her own shop in Manhattan.

Ursula was the executive producer of 15 of Bob Hope's USO Christmas tours which included close association with Jill St. John, Danny Kaye, Mickey Mantle (she said he was "gross") Jerry Colonna,

Raquel Welch, Brooke Shields and many more. Ursula knew everyone *important* as we'd bump into Steve and Edie at one club… Jackie Gleason at another, usually Toots Shor's.

When she started her own PR operation in New York, she already had clients such as Johnson & Johnson, NBC, General Motors Pontiac Division, Victor Borge, Shari Lewis and the Reynolds Metals account.

At the end of my fruitful day lining up magazine stories for our upcoming show, I went to her office to say hello and casually mentioned that I had a pretty good day. I had commitments from publications totaling 16 million readers. It seemed to shake her up.

I imagined she was thinking, "Who the hell is this guy from the Chicago ad agency scoring big on my turf with *my* client?"

She was a real pro and knew the game well. So when "Do It Yourself" debuted in that coveted NBC 7:00 p.m. time slot, she augmented my PR effort by obtaining the **covers** of the entertainment sections of the *New York Times* and the *New York Herald Tribune*. Over 10 million readers. *Touché.*

Several months later Ursula attempted to get me to join her company, which would involve moving to New York. I told her *no way* could I tell the home front I'm working for a gorgeous, high-powered public relations chick in rock 'em, sock 'em fast-paced New York City.

That would not go well with a wife and two little kids all firmly ensconced in Chicago suburbia.

Visiting glamorous New York City with an unlimited expense account every few weekends, staying at the St. Regis and the Plaza was a far cry when three years later I actually moved to Gotham and saw the real Madison Avenue of cold shoulders, ruthlessness and many tongues.

A near disaster on live network TV

When "Mr. Peepers" returned to the air in the fall, I was back to commuting weekends to New York to keep the client happy. And that's when it all almost exploded in my face. Or at least in Helen Lewis' face.

Helen did the Reynolds Wrap cooking and recipe spots. Between the dress rehearsal and the live show, we had to keep an eye on the crew to keep them from eating the food she was cooking or screwing around with our props.

Commercial production cast and crew of "Mr. Peepers," starring Wally Cox and Tony Randall, takes a bow after live NBC broadcast of the show. As Reynolds Metals Account Executive, I got to join in the fun before the live studio audience (I'm 7th from right, back row).

One Sunday night, as she was in the middle of a barbecue demonstration, the grill became an inferno… flames five feet high erupted… almost singeing Helen. Someone had put a quart of starter fluid in the grill. And we were LIVE… NBC coast-to-coast. Helen became unglued.

Luckily, Reynolds TV commercial spokesman Rex Marshall, with his deep soothing voice, stepped in and saved the day. He took the steak off the grill with some handy prongs and said, "Here, Helen… let me take care of this for you.

Reynolds Metals spokesman, Rex Marshall, well known in advertising and TV circles in the 50's and 60's, was Reynolds spokesman for many years.

Rex was adept at "saving" live TV commercial faux pas situations as he was the Maxwell House Coffee TV presenter widely known as the poor soul who "broke the glass coffee cup" on camera while pouring from a carafe.

Helen gave him a weird look and continued her pitch. She was really shaken up after the show as she told us, "Jeez… I thought it was a rehearsal and I was about to say, "Rex, keep your f ****** hands off my steak."

Helen went out and had four martinis at nearby El Borracho Bistro, home of the world renowned Kiss Room where 1,000 celebs left kiss samples on the walls. She finally came down to earth, safe in the knowledge that while the grill blew up, her career didn't.

My favorite zinger… on ice!

In 1956, Reynolds Aluminum decided it wanted to sponsor a figure skating TV special. Big time figure skating had originated in 1892, then became a popular worldwide Olympic sport. It spawned super skaters Dorothy Hamill, Scott Hamilton, Nancy Kerrigan and Dick Button. However, it wasn't until the early days of television that a national audience was formally introduced to the colorful and demanding sport. Norway's Sonja Henie firmly established figure skating as a big-ticket sporting event.

Sonja Henie was a major motion picture star and Olympic figure skating champion when she signed to headline one of the very first NBC network television color specials. Her 1956 "Holiday on Ice" show was to originate from the new Brooklyn studios of NBC where the network had constructed an ice skating rink specifically designed for this December 1956 TV special. My client Reynolds Metals, happily agreed to sponsor the Sunday prime time show. I went to Brooklyn to work on commercials and watch Ms. Henie perform.

Sonja Henie was on her toes around me.

Why the three-time Olympic champion felt she needed to do strenuous figure skating routines for television was beyond me. Her movie salary was $200,000. She was married to a billionaire businessman Dan Topping, owner of the New York Yankees baseball team. She headlined a Madison Square Garden ice show.

Before I arrived to supervise the commercials, I had heard the rumors of her imperious behavior. She allowed only one person to sharpen her skates and had him take a train from Chicago to the Big Apple just to perform that 30-minute chore. Then he went back the Windy City. Ms. Henie told people her goal was to be "Fred Astaire on ice!"

I went to the Brooklyn studios to check out rehearsals and block out my commercials for the one-hour TV show. I looked forward to meeting *The Queen of the Ice*. To everyone's amazement there was no Sonja. There was a full network television production crew, 20 male and female skaters, other talent, client representatives and the director… but no Sonja. We all sat around for well over an hour waiting for the *Queen* to arrive as the show budget clock was ticking away.

She finally made her entrance and the show's director tore into the Scandinavian seductress telling her how unprofessional she was keeping everyone waiting and being late. She flared up, sat him down and spat out that she was a star, told him that in no way would he criticize her and she would perform on her terms. He better shape up or she would leave. *Fini*. We were all in shock.

The woman was a real *bitch*.

Finally, rehearsals began and we were again amazed as Ms. Henie, now in her mid-40s, decided that in Saturday rehearsals she would not do the more strenuous spins, spirals and arabesques (no big-time jumping was allowed then) until air time… game day. She said she was a Sunday player.

On Sunday, "Holiday on Ice" with Ms. Sonja Henie aired live on the NBC TV Network without a hitch. She did a good job even though she distanced herself from everyone in the cast and crew, acting like the *queen bee*.

After the show, the client and I went back to her dressing room where she sat looking haggard and spent. Her makeup was smeared all over her face and she gave us two minutes of her valuable time.

Still a bitch.

Two hours later we were at the King Cole Room of the St. Regis Hotel with the client, Jack Boyle of Reynolds Metals, my ad agency boss, Wade Grinstead and TV public relations heavyweight Ursula Halloran discussing the TV show and, of course, Ms. Henie. Sonja Henie.

Someone asked, "What makes that broad such a bitch?"
And I replied, "Probably **Tight Skates**." *My zinger.*

Stop the presses! *My one ad that really stunk!*

One of my accounts was Curtiss Candy Company who manufactured about 100 confections besides Baby Ruth and Butterfinger candy bars. They make Halloween specialties, Christmas candy, malted milk balls and much more. In an effort to grab a share of the huge Kool-Aid market, Curtis produced a powdered drink called Flavor Aid, a Kool-Aid knockoff.

I thought it would be a unique marketing ploy and distribution-getter as well as a cool taste test program to actually put a sample three-ounce envelope of the stuff in a regional section of TV Guide, Americas No.1 weekly consumer magazine. The advertising rep for TV Guide liked the idea and sent packages to his press people in Radnor, Pennsylvania.

It was a very competitive time for media ad dollars and media people were willing to take chances. *TV Guide,* thinking the very expensive test would lead to a *big* ad contract from my client, thought it was a bit crazy but possibly *do-able.* They gave it a test shot in a regional edition covering part of Indiana.

WOW! What a publicity-getting debacle. Even though we pulled it off and thousands of people received free samples of Flavor Aid, the test was a production nightmare. Everything *smelled* of grape drink... the printing presses in Radnor jammed up... newsstands everywhere stunk... grape odor permeated mailrooms all over the Hoosier state... post offices reeked of grape.

Obviously we did not take this test national. It was a one-shot publicity campaign and definitely was not doable, but it was unique. I'm told the printing plant in Radnor still smells grapey.

Stop the presses again!
My one ad that foiled the newspaper industry!

After the Flavor Aid TV Guide insert seemed to lay an egg, I saw another off-the-wall Reynolds Metals promotional idea get tanked.

Thankfully.

The Reynolds Brothers, Billy, David and Louis, were open to crazy advertising ideas. They were innovators and were willing to manufacture almost anything out of aluminum.

ANYTHING!

In fact, a joke going around Reynolds executive dining room, the *Alumadrome,* about the colorful brothers, went like this:

Billy Reynolds: "Why don't we make aluminum golf clubs?

Dave Reynolds: "Great idea… how many sets should we make?"

Billy: "Well there are a hundred million men in the U.S., so we make a hundred million sets."

Dave: "Sure… why not."

When the company bean counters got into the act, no golf clubs were ever produced but it illustrates the highly creative and fairly zany atmosphere that prevailed at Reynolds Metals in Louisville, Kentucky.

We at the ad agency really loved it, as our client was always open to new ideas.

One time we ran a full-page newspaper ad in the *Milwaukee Journal* for Reynolds Wrap and printed the page on Reynolds aluminum foil. It was sensational but too expensive to run in additional newspapers.

But it did cause a stir in the ad world showing that our ad agency could think "out of the box." Reynolds was a client that would listen to new ideas… ones that would make a PR impact.

Reynolds Wrap and the "Reynollettes" …
If a pretty woman can fix it…"

Another concept I came up with for Reynolds was the "Reynollettes." Reynolds had a very active consumer products division that catered to the do-it-yourself home handy man via products sold through hardware stores and homebuilder outlets.

Called "Reynolds Do-It-Yourself" Aluminum Products," it consisted of large displays of Reynolds aluminum strips, sheets and extrusions of all sorts that enable the average man-about-the-house to actually make his own window screens, storm windows, shelves, gutters, garden items and 1000 other applications. I even made the screens and storm windows for my house in Prospect Heights, Illinois.

This was a whole new marketing problem… educating people to the ease of using Reynolds Do-It-Yourself Aluminum for a variety of home repairs and upgrades.

It was "strong, lightweight, rustproof and you can cut it with a common hacksaw or cut sheets with mother's scissors… easy to use and saves you from hiring expensive contractors."

We ran a great many print ads in men's magazines, did a few TV commercials and hardware store distribution rolled out nationally.

But we still had a teaching job confronting us for not only the end user consumer but for the store clerks.

One day, after watching a comely female model demonstrate men's electric shavers on a TV talk show, I hatched the idea of organizing a team of a dozen female demonstrators to go out to various markets and put on do-it-yourself product demonstrations… actually make storm windows, screens, whatever.

The idea obviously directed at the home handyman was, "If a pretty woman can make these things… so can you!"

Note: This wasn't exactly the most politically correct time…
but no one cared then!

I suggested hiring a team of airline stewardesses (that's what they were called at the time), give them "Reynollette" uniforms, train them on the use of Reynolds products and have the public relations department turn them loose in major markets, TV talk show demonstrations, trade shows and organizations are always in search of speakers for their monthly meetings... A sure-fire publicity-getter.

My boss loved the idea and immediately called Dave Reynolds and said, "Bill has a super idea for the Do-It-Yourself Aluminum program. He'll be in Louisville day after tomorrow."

I presented it with a budget and even sketches of the "Reynollette" uniforms. The Reynolds guys loved it but after thorough consideration they passed on it saying they thought a team of good-looking ladies roaming the country could possibly spell trouble for the corporation.

They did have a point and I should have recommended a pilot test program... but did not. Anyway, we made more brownie points with our client.

A Reynolds Wrap business lunch

The CEO of Reynolds Metals was David Reynolds, a Yale classmate of Clint Frank.

He was scheduled to be the keynote luncheon speaker for the American Marketing Association convention held at The Palmer House in Chicago. Clint wanted this 1958 event to be a first class affair, not only for the purpose of impressing our client but to also introduce our ad agency to dozens of the top advertising executives in Chicagoland.

He assigned me to get together with AMA Executive Director Dick Revnes to make sure Mr. Reynolds appearance would be memorable. Revnes was my age and a real dynamo; smart, engaging and authoritive. We worked well together. I had the 400 luncheon meeting invites printed on aluminum foil in a six inch miniature Reynolds Wrap box and mailed to all the AMA members.

Tableware at each place setting were aluminum utensils.
Baked potato was wrapped in (what else?) Reynolds Aluminum
Foil, and lastly dessert consisted of delicious Eskimo Pie ice
cream bars, which came foil-wrapped. Reynolds owned the
Eskimo Pie Company.

The luncheon was a great success and our client was happy.
Clint was happy and later that evening we all went to a suite at
the Yale Club for drinks and the Yalies played Cribbage.
Cribbage? I'm from the Big Ten and I was lost.
But it was a good day.

*The Empire Room at the Palmer House Chicago where the
AMA Reynolds luncheon took place.*

CHAPTER THREE

Here's Jonnie Winters… my time with this
mad, mad, mad, mad comedian

It was 1955 in Hollywood that I first met Jonnie.

Jonnie had just been "recognized" in New York, intending to do only network radio, but the TV world quickly discovered him. He left his hometown of Dayton where he had worked as a radio personality.

If I had known Jonnie was going to be such a big star I would have made sure I had a better picture of the two of us together.

I was staying at the Hollywood Roosevelt Hotel for a week, working on Reynolds Metals television commercials for an upcoming NBC network television special, a variety show titled "Remember 1938," hosted by Groucho Marx and featuring Ethel Barrymore, Oscar Levant and 1938 newsmaker, football star Douglas "Wrong Way" Corrigan.

Also to appear was the new, upcoming comic, who was making big noise on popular TV shows… Jonathan Winters.

I first met Jonnie at the Roosevelt's bar.

Of course, of course, for both of us.

As it turned out, our hotel rooms were next to each other. We were close to the same age, and we were both wired for fun and frolic.

We hit it off immediately, especially when Jonnie looked into the huge mirror behind the bar and found out the room we were in was populated wall-to-wall by women.

All kinds. Lots of them. The Roosevelt was home base for a national convention of cosmetologists and Winters quickly figured it was a candy store.

"I'll have one of those, two of those and two of those."

As I watched his reflection in the mirrored wall behind the bar, Jonnie got up and wandered around the room packed with *interesting* women from all over the U.S.

I couldn't hear what he said to them but I could read his lips as he kept asking, "Are you horny?"

Wow… I don't believe this. Then he motioned, "C'mon over… they're horny."

So we had a chat… and that was that… because in situations like this Jonnie was all talk, no action and he entertained us for an hour as he practiced his TV routines.

Winters created a great many unique and odd personalities:

Maude Frickert, Lamont G. Lamont, Elwood P. Suggins and Willis Mumford. My favorite was the spin on John Wayne's sidekick, Ward Bond, the perennial boss of a dozen Western movies about wagon trains.

Circle the wagons… Jonnie's about to perform …

Jonnie instantly turned on his magic for the beauticians. As he started this wildly funny routine, I really believed I was there.

Scenario: A wagon train is attacked by "Injuns" and Winters does several characters including the Wagon Master ("Make a circle of the wagons!"); Miss Ellie, who is scared and screams; young wrangler Little Joey, who has never shot a gun.

"I think I got one... I got one," the wagon train's cook is yelling.

Winters makes sound effects of bullets, whizzing arrows and screams. Suddenly... all is eerily silent... the "Injun" raid is over. Then we hear Jonnie doing his musical interpretation of a bugle... just blaring away... completely unintelligible, non-related, jumbled-up horn notes.

The marauding Indian Chief says, *"Not bad... first time play white man horn."*

> *Jonnie was the show ... wherever we went ...*
> *he was always on*

Jonnie was just starting to receive national recognition via guest shots network TV. NBC seemed to be grooming him for bigger things and he later went on to appear often on Jack Parr, Johnny Carson and so many more variety shows. He was "being noticed."
He was starting to do a lot of nightclubs as well.

We decided that after working rehearsals we would explore places of interest in LA-LA land.

We went out every night for almost a week, and I don't know how we got any work done, but we did. Winters *was* the show everywhere we partied. He was always on.

In fact, whenever he came to Chicago in later years he would be the star attraction at some of our favorite watering holes. Scotch was his favorite libation.

The NBC-TV special with Winters was a hit. He and I agreed that after the cast-client party we'd meet at the Brown Derby to go out and have some fun. In fact, he said, we may have some new "friends."

Hmmm.

We did meet up, but it was only for about 15 minutes. He had just received a call from his agent in New York excitedly telling him "get back here to New York immediately. You were such a hit on tonight's show the NBC brass want to give you your very own network TV show. We meet tomorrow morning, to discuss a new 15 minute weekly Jonathan Winters TV show."

That, of course, was fantastic news.

The insanity of Jonnie... funny... creative... bizarre

The morning sun was peeking through the clouds over the double-ugly Hollywood Sign south of L.A. By cab, Jonnie and I were headed to the Hollywood Roosevelt Hotel on Hollywood Boulevard. We had just done an all-night party... third in a row... somebody's manse in Beverly Hills and, of course, Winters was the main attraction.

Though the party we were returning from at this ungodly hour was a fun lampshade-on-head bash, we had to face the grim fact we were going to work sans sleep. Winters had rehearsals at the El Capitan Theater. I had to go to the NBC studios in Burbank to block out several live TV commercials for Reynolds Metals; one of which included a monstrous airplane wing, and, of course, our cooking demonstrations using Reynolds wrap.

A Little Austin Healey sports car pulled alongside our cab. I told Jonnie that I had one just like that back home in Chicago and it was being customized to look like a baby Aston Martin.

As soon as I said Austin Healey, Winters went ballistic. He got all tensed up and said "Bill, never ever say those words to me again... Never say Austin Healey. I don't want to hear the words Austin Healey. Please no Austin Healey. My loving brother... my only brother... died in an Austin Healey."

"Geez, I'm sorry," I said.

"It was his high school graduation party and my folks gave him a new Austin Healey sports car. He got boozed up and decided to play race driver through the mountains near where we lived in Ohio," Jonnie said tearfully. "He took a curve too fast, flipped, rolled down the mountain caught fire and was burned to death. Geez I don't want think about... horrible."

"Wow Jonnie. I'm sorry. Jesus, no more Austin Healey's... promise," I said while wondering about the tall peaks in Ohio.

Fast-forward two weeks later

I was in New York City having lunch with the unit manager for our Peabody Award winning TV series, *"Mr. Peepers."* The unit manager was Reynolds Metals TV commercial employee, John Calley. Yes that John Calley… the guy who became CEO of Sony Pictures.

A unit manager for a television production is sort of a clerical job, and he's the guy that keeps track of all the bits and pieces and primarily the money mechanics of a production. I was meeting with Calley because we had a warehouse full of Reynolds Metals TV commercial props… car parts, swimming pools, outdoor grills and much more, in a Brooklyn warehouse. I wanted to dump the stuff… lose the storage fee. It didn't take me 20 minutes rapping with Calley to realize he was not going to be a unit manager for long. He was destined for bigger things in the TV business. He seemed to know everybody in show business. He also seemed to be very real, and like me, he was a car nut. In fact, years later, I learned he was one of the biggest collectors of Ferraris in the US.

Calley knew Jonnie Winters. As I said, Calley knew everybody so as we talked cars, specifically, sports cars, I told him about my cars: MGTD, Simca, Austin Healey and the crazy scene I had with Winters about his brother being burned to death in a Healey.

Calley says, "Bill, Winters does not have a brother. He's an only child. I've been to his parent's house in Dayton, Ohio. I know his parents. He does not, and did not have a brother."

I knew Jonnie Winters was a bit odd… but this was *bizarre.*

Jonnie's rotten agent vs. his good agent

Immediately after our Hollywood capers and Winters' great appearance on the NBC-TV special, I hooked up with him in New York. I was staying at the Warwick Hotel near NBC and Jonnie's agent at the time, Syd Weinberg, had an office in that hotel.

My agency was about to make a pitch for the $1 million Four Fisherman seafood account. I thought Winters, with all his characters, would be a natural for a couple TV commercials. He could do a take-off of all of the Four Fisherman voices… Jonnie liked it. It would probably pay him $100,000. It would be a good gig for him

We took the idea to Syd and he turned it down. He gave us some lame excuse about Winters not doing commercials. I really thought it was because we, Clinton E. Frank Advertising was, compared to the major NYC ad agencies, relatively unknown, and we were in Chicago, not the Big Apple. I was peeved and so was Winters.

Soon after that, Winters dumped Weinberg and hired Hollywood agent George Spota. They had a great 30-year relationship. I got along very well with George.

He was in his own world… not always a good place

Jonnie was flying high – literally and figuratively – for a number of years but he was always his own worst enemy. One night he apparently flipped out and was caught and jailed for climbing the rigging of a tall ship in the San Francisco harbor. After this, he went through a career gap in a mental institution.

Incredibly enough he often made light of his days in the mental institution, referring to it as the "loony bin" or the "zoo."

He told me that as a kid, he used to stay in his room and perfect sound effects. I took it that he didn't have a very happy childhood and later his parents divorced. He particularly liked imitating auto races, which, of course, endeared me to him.

It was pretty tough for him to get steady work but I thought he was the greatest, and I looked for opportunities for him to further showcase his remarkable talent.

I helped him get re-established… he did the rest

I was in charge of entertainment for a national automotive club convention at the Conrad Hilton in Chicago, and I convinced the club execs that Jonathan Winters should be the headliner. They set a budget and said, "Go get him." And I did.

His fee included a room at the Hilton and expenses. I kept sending him notes containing all sorts of information about sports cars that he might want to incorporate in his appearance. Turns out he ignored all my input but was still a hit.

When he came into O'Hare Field with his agent George Spota, I picked him up with my pal Bill Contos, owner of one of Chicago's poshest restaurants, Chez Paul, in Bill's brand new Cadillac convertible.

Chez Paul on North Rush Street, corner of Erie and Rush, was a favorite watering hole for ad types. Owner Bill Contos always joined in the fun.

Winters was impressed. I told him that I got him a suite; a better hotel than the Hilton. He would be staying at the St. Regis. Now the finest hotel in New York is the St. Regis so naturally Jonnie figured we were really going first class for him. What he didn't know is that in Chicago the St. Regis is a dollar-a-day flophouse on Chicago's North Clark Street's skid row. It's grim… a place where the drunks sit on the sidewalk sipping on a bottle of wine.

We drove in from O'Hare taking the scenic routes and suddenly hit skid row where we opened the door let Jonnie and George out with their bags and said "bye." Now they're on skid row... confused... pissed off. Of course, we went around the block came back and picked him up. He and George were sizzling mad as they were surrounded by drunken homeless people.

We took him to the Hilton where two days later Winters brought the house down as he started with "I drive a 1938 Studebaker with Ferrari tires..."

His popularity caught on and he was immediately hired by the Art Director's Club of Chicago to come back a month later and do a repeat of the Hilton performance this time at the Blackstone Hotel.

A month later, he came back to the Windy City to do two weeks at the popular Rush Street night club, The Black Orchid, where he confessed to me he'd better clean up his act as his wife Elaine was threatening to leave him.

He did shape up... *(cut out the booze).*

It looked to me like he was back in business and maybe I helped a bit.

Jonnie's back in town… and starts a unique "club"

Jonnie kept dropping in and out of my life over the years. In 1959, he was in town doing his gig at The Black Orchid and we had lunch at Chez Paul. The restaurant owner, Bill Contos, who was about the same age as Winters and me, and a very outgoing personality, really hit it off with Winters. They'd do animated chats in foreign tongues that they'd make up on the spot. People thought they both were nuts as they ranted on with absolutely no idea what the other guy was saying and it was a free floor show.

After lunch, I had to go back to work at my ad agency office in the Merchandise Mart. Winters said he'd meet me later at the Mart's major saloon, Henrici's, a huge, popular watering hole in the world's largest office building, owned by the Kennedy clan.

We were drinking Brandy Alexander's and Jonnie thought it would be fun to invite some of the gals from my company, Clinton E. Frank Advertising, down to the bar for a quick drink… all of them… one at a time.

There was a phone at the bar. We'd call a secretary, then a bookkeeper, and on and on. He said, "Come on down to Henrici's if you want to join the 'Horny Club.'"

At least eight female employees showed up and asked, "How do I join the Horny Club?"

He'd say to each one, "Easy… just be horny."

Believe it or not, it was a very innocent afternoon and the gals were thrilled to meet network television's newest comic who was on a roll at that time.

Another time at the Wrigley Bar with his pal, funny guy Pat McCormick, the two of them decided to create an act where Pat was a German U-boat skipper attacking a British destroyer captained by Winters… all in the correct dialects. It was so crazy I actually fell off a bar stool laughing.

It was a *Mad, Mad, Mad, Mad World* that night… a good eight years before MGM featured Winters with Milton Berle and Shelley Winters in a movie of that title.

I began to conclude that life on the road was rough for him. He became unglued a number of times (more than has been publicized) and was institutionalized. He was really was just a small town boy who wanted to go home.

He was a "rotten" Marine

Jonathan Winters had been a Marine. "A *rotten* Marine" is the way he put it. He screwed up at every Marine base where he was stationed and that included the stockade. He kept giving the brass a bunch of crap and they gave it right back to him and he never earned a promotion.

That story changed when he became a headline. The United States Marine Corps suddenly loved the guy. They paid him handsomely to entertain at Marine bases.

At his house in Hastings-on-Hudson, New York, he showed me a beautiful chrome inscribed officer's sword the Marine Corps gave to him in appreciation. He thought that was a real hoot. Jar-head Marine screw-up gets big-time Marine recognition.

And he was a real hoot…

And speaking of hoots, Winter's main hobby was owls. Yes. Owls. He had some kind of inner feeling about owls. In fact, he invested some money in a retail store off Fifth Avenue in the Big Apple that was devoted strictly to owls… stuffed owls, owl paintings, owl games, owl movies and owl costumes. Weird.

The one day I was a bigger star than Jonnie

Winters headed for the big time and Hollywood and our paths seldom crossed. I believe one reason was he attempted to distance himself from a few acquaintances due to an "unwritten" Alcoholics Anonymous credo to "divest yourself of your drinking buddies." Just a guess.

 I did bump into him in 1973 at the monthly luncheon of The Hollywood Radio and Television Society held at the Beverly Hilton where he was speaking.

We had a subdued chat about old friends including my former New York pal, comedy writer Jim Lehner with whom I shared a huge 56th street apartment in New York City that overlooked the Town Tennis Club where we watched Ginger Rogers lob tennis balls.

This luncheon was interesting. My actor/film producer pal George Carey ("General Hospital," "Ironside," "Gomer Pyle," "Weekend with the Babysitter") invited me to sit at his table.

All of a sudden the emcee said "And we have a special guest here today from the East Coast… former agency producer for the Peabody award-winning NBC-TV series, 'Mr. Peepers,'… Bill Maloney."

It was nice. I received an unexpected standing ovation. Jonnie wasn't the only star that day.

P.S. on Jonnie…

One of the most unforgettable characters of my life

I never saw him after 1973, but we had a hell of a time in earlier years. The guy was no less than brilliant. His imagination, delivery, timing, wit and creativity were unequalled.

In his later years in Santa Barbara, California, he painted and was featured at many art shows.

There were reports that he went to the bank every day in Santa Barbara and on a good day would entertain the tellers.

His family owned the Winters Bank in Dayton. He felt comfortable at the bank.

===========

R.I.P. April 12, 2013.

===========

CHAPTER FOUR

The biggest side gig of all… and my proudest patriotic moment… the captured German U-505 submarine comes to Chicago

A few years earlier at Foote Cone and Belding, I landed an even bigger side gig… my U-505 project.

One day in 1954, I was slaving over a script for a Meadow Gold Ranch Sunday afternoon kids TV show I was producing at WGN-TV for our client Meadow Gold Dairies.

Admiral Dan Gallery calls… again. He changes my life.

I received a phone call and the caller said, "Maloney, this is Dan Gallery."

Admiral Dan Gallery was then head of U.S. Naval Air Reserve and Commander at Glenview Naval Air Station in a northern Chicago suburb. Admirals never called enlisted men like me by their first name.

The Admiral said, "Maloney, we're bringing the U-505 captured German submarine into Chicago from Portsmouth, Rhode Island, and I want you on the team to head publicity. You owe me one."

And I did. He had changed my life once. He was about to do it again.

Forgetting I had been a civilian since that time, I came to attention and said, "Yes, sir!"

"I'll send a car for you tomorrow afternoon to pick you up at your work place and get you out to Glenview. I'll tell you exactly what I need," he said in his authoritative admiral's voice. You don't argue with admirals.

I have to admit it was pretty cool the next day at 5:00 p.m., leaving the FC&B building on Ontario Street at Michigan Avenue, with dozens of other co-workers, and a uniformed U.S. Navy sailor stood at attention holding the door open for me. A U.S. Navy admiral's car was waiting… for me, and it had four stars on the license plate.

The German U-505 submarine story…
and a true American hero

Now this story isn't my story. It's my old family friend Admiral Dan Gallery's story. I only played a small part in his big story.

My dad was great friends with Dan from their Chicago Catholic school days. It was that family connection that got me transferred from that hell hole post in Nevada during World War II to the comparative luxury of the S.S. Minnow!

Dan Gallery was a wiry, 140-pound U.S. Naval Academy grad, an Olympic wrestler, competing at age 19 in the 1920 Antwerp Games. While at the Academy in Annapolis he devised a scheme to capture an enemy man-of-war; that is, if he ever got the opportunity.

He had a vivid imagination (in later years he authored 12 books on baseball and naval warfare) and he steadfastly fine-tuned his enemy capture plan.

He spent most of his pre-war career as a naval aviator and was the Naval Attaché to the U.S. Embassy in London when our country entered the war.

Early in the conflict the Germans were wearing us out with their submarines. Their U-Boats – the German name for a submarine – controlled the Atlantic, sinking battleships and merchant ships alike. In 1943 alone U-boats sank more than 1,400 ships.

To fight back, the U.S Navy created the anti-submarine Task Group 21.12 with Captain Dan Gallery in charge. The group's mission was to hunt down U-boats and sink them.

But Captain Dan had another idea; an idea he had had since his days in the Naval Academy. He wanted to capture an enemy craft. When he was placed in charge of the Hunter-Killer Task Group 22.3 he created an elite boarding group that could land on an enemy U-boat before it could be scuttled.

And thus began an inevitable collision course between Captain Dan's TFG 22.3 and the German submarine U-505.

By the spring of 1944, U-505 had been in service for two years and in that time patrolling the Atlantic it had sunk eight ships, three of them American. But her time was running out.

In late May the Navy dispatched Task Group 22.3 to the area around Cape Verde in the central Atlantic, where intelligence indicated a group of U-boats were operating.

On Sunday, June 4, 1944, two days before the Allied Invasion of Normandy in World War II, Captain Gallery and his group consisting of the baby flattop U.S.S. Guadalcanal and five destroyer escorts steamed off the coast of French West Africa.

Gallery was about to get his chance for a capture. He had his prize crew – electricians, engineers, gunners, torpedo men and boatswain's mates plus a film camera operator – were at the ready.

In late morning the sonar operator on the Destroyer Chatelain, DE-149 reported a ping some 800 yards off the starboard bow.

It was U-505.

The chase was on.

Captain Gallery backed his aircraft carrier Guadalcanal away at top speed in order to launch an air attack.

Soon there were three fighters in the air, two Grumman Wildcats and an Avenger, each honing in on the target. Meanwhile the Chatelain was firing Hedgehog mortars and following them up with depth charges.

Then came the message from the air, "You struck oil! Sub is surfacing!"

An oil slick was forming and in the center was the bridge of the U-505 emerging from the water.

When water began flooding into the sub, U-505 commander Oberleutnant Harald Lange ordered his men to abandon ship and the 59 sailors were clamoring up through the conning tower.

Capt. Gallery knew this was his chance to capture a fully equipped U-boat and ordered his fighter planes to cease bombing and his vessels to use only small artillery fire, 20 and 50 mm guns and anti-personnel ammunition.

That was when Gallery gave the historic order, "Away, All Boarders," an order not used since the War of 1812, when an American Naval party from the Wasp captured the British Frolic. An eight-man boarding party from the escort Pillsbury took off for the U-505.

To scuttle a U-boat and send it to the bottom of the ocean was a three-step procedure and involved opening the sea strainer and the scuttling valves, both designed to allow seawater to enter the vessel, and arming 14 detonation charges.

The men of the boarding party quickly closed the scuttling valves and reinstalled the sea strainer cap, gathering charts and codebooks as they disarmed 13 of the detonators. But there was a 14th detonator located in the rudder room.

A crewman locked the door behind him, so any explosion would be contained in that area, and proceeded to unlock the rudder and remove the final detonator.

U-505 captured by Task Group 22.3, June 4, 1944

U.S. Colors fly over captured U-505

The U-505 had been captured, the first foreign man-of-war captured on the high seas (by the U.S.) in 132 years.

When the boarding party did a full sweep of the sub, they uncovered a treasure trove of intelligence, including two Enigma coding machines. Those coding devices would allow the Allies to break Germany's secret codes and decode war messages without the Nazi's knowing.

Proving, as if it needed proving, that no good deed goes unpunished, Captain Gallery was given a thorough dressing down by his commanding officer, Admiral Ernest J. King, Chief of Naval Operations. King considered the operation pointless because the Germans would learn about the capture and immediately change the codes.

And here may be the most remarkable part of the operation:

Captain Gallery convinced his men of the need for secrecy. The U-boat was towed secretly to the Bahamas, where it rode out the rest of the war. And the German prisoners were taken to Louisiana where they were imprisoned by themselves and denied access to the Red Cross and other relief organizations.

The German populace was told that their sub had been sunk and all aboard killed. And American and British intelligence officers could read secret German messages with impunity. End of story, at least for ten years. That's when I re-enter the picture with that phone call from now-Admiral Gallery.

After the War, the U-505 sub had been taken to Portsmouth, Rhode Island where it sat molding until Dan Gallery, now Admiral Gallery, along with the Chicago Chapter of the Navy League of the United States decided that this would make a great monument to the heroism of Americans sailors. The capture was engineered by a Chicagoan and should be ensconced in The Chicago Museum of Science and History.

> *I'm appointed head of publicity for the sub's Chicago appearance*

I'm thinking, "I've come a long way from the ammunition dump in Hell, Nevada eight years before… to handling publicity for one of the most important U.S. Navy events ever." Thanks, again, to Admiral Dan Gallery.

So in that infamous 1954 phone conversation, Gallery said to me, "Maloney we're bringing the U-505 Submarine into Chicago from Portsmouth, Rhode Island, and I want you on the team to head publicity. You owe me one."

I dug in and started working with a Chicago Navy vet, David Jenkins, who was a member of the prize crew, scheduling media interviews for him and Admiral Gallery on all the major TV and radio shows.

We also organized fundraisers as we got the City of Chicago "Submarine Conscious." We had a game plan; it was successful as we raised $250,000, which in today's dollars is over $2 million to bring the German U-505 to Chicago.

*One of those guys on the deck of the U-505 is **me**. Just can't figure out which one!*
The U.S. Navy Band played, the Secretary of the Navy spoke and thousands cheered.
It was a heckuva celebration; the emotional high point of which, at least in my mind, was
seeing the remaining members of the original U.S. Navy crew standing on the deck of
the dreaded German "untersee boot." Ten years before that, they risked their lives.
They were waving to their wives and young children on the dock all whom
were wearing U-505 Navy caps.

I'll never forget the big day, June 26, 1954 and the Secretary of the Navy. The U-505 was towed from Lake Michigan, past Navy Pier, through the Chicago River locks and docked in front of the Michigan Avenue Bridge.

Visualize a bunch of small kids pointing at the U-Boat and saying, "That's my pop. He captured a German submarine." It was a proud day and a fulfilling moment … Lump in my throat…

Two days later the sub was towed south in Lake Michigan toward its final resting place, The Chicago Museum of Science & Industry where it has been viewed by millions of people since its arrival.

At 3:00 a.m. on a Monday morning, it was rolled across South Lake Shore Drive to the Museum.

With auto traffic stopped in all directions some prankster, possibly a news photographer, put a sign up on South Shore Drive that said, "DRIVE CAREFULLY SUBMARINE CROSSING." No, it was not me. Although that was the sort of prank I would have pulled at U of I, not that many years earlier.

I spent years trying to hunt down the original sign. Just recently I found it at the Woodlawn Tap in the Hyde Park neighborhood of Chicago.

I am honored to say that my name is an appreciation plaque at the Museum of Science and Industry along with the Illinois Governor, Chicago Mayor, U.S. Senator and Navy League Officers who formed the U-505 Museum Committee.

There would be many more wildly interesting side gigs coming up... to say the least!

The U-505 as it looks today at the Museum of Science and Industry.

1954 U-505 Submarine Memorial Exhibit Committee

Ralph A. Bard,
Honorary Chairman

Robert Crown,
Committee Co-Chairman

Carl Stockholm,
Committee Co-Chairman

Ex-Officio Members

William G. Stratton,
Governor Of Illinois

Everett M. Dirksen,
United States Senator

Paul M. Douglas,
United States Senator

Martin H. Kennelly
Mayor Of Chicago

Robert McCormick Adams	J.B. Kolka
Charles W. Allen	Francis H. Kullman, Jr.
Ralph L. Atlass, Jr.	William A. Lee
A.G. Cox Atwater	George W. Lennon
Charles W. Becker	Louis E. Leverone
Louis J. Behan	D.M. MacNamara
Carl A. Birdsall	William Maloney
A. Andrew Boemi	John L. Maloney
P.P. Brautigam	J.L. McCaffrey
Mark A. Brown	Joseph J. McCarthy
Maurice F. Brown	F.B. McConnell
Fred J. Byington, Jr.	James G. McDonald
John L. Clarkson	John F. McGuire
Edward D. Corboy	Dr. L. Robert Mellin
Thomas A. Dean	Gerhardt F. Mayne
John L. Donoghue	Edward F. Misewicz
William W. Downey	Raymond T. Maloney
Alex Dreier	Vice Admiral Francis P. Old, USN (Ret)
Brian J. Ducey	Lieutenant E.W. Oliphant, USNR
T.M. Dunlap	Rudolph F. Onsrud
Lee Ettelson	W.A. Patterson
T.J. Ellecthorpe Ync, USN	Harold E. Peterson
John W. Evers	Ken Regan
Harold S. Falk	Rear Admiral James M. Ross, USNR
John D. Farrington	Willard M. Rutzen
James B. Forgan	Brigadier General E.H. Salzman
Jack Foster	Philip B. Schnering
B.T. Franck	Rudolph A. Schoenecker
Philip Furlong	Gilbert H. Scribner
Reverend John I. Gallery	Sherman H. Serre
Arthur Godfrey	James G. Shakman
David N. Goldenson	Rear Admiral D.F.J. Shea
Seth M. Gooder	Arnold Sobel
James R. Graham	John L. Spicsak
Leonard H. Groose	Russ Stewart
Cornelius J. Hagan	Arthur Sullivan
Morton Hogue	Patrick F. Sullivan
George S. Halas	Hamilton Vose, Jr.
David L. Harrington	Basil L. Walters
Edward A. Hayes	William P. Wholen
Frank A. Hecht	John A. Wheeler
Maurice L. Horner, Jr.	Roger Q. White
Oscar Iber	Thomas F. White, Jr.
	Lawrence H. Whiting

I'm proud to have my name on this plaque at the U-505 exhibit.

CHAPTER FIVE

The Windy City Ad Man in Me

I love "Mad Men," AMC's cable TV series about New York ad men in the 1960's, but I don't love the way it portrays ad men as always drinking in the office.

In Chicago we didn't have bars in the office. Hell, we had to walk down the street to a real bar to get a martini, the drink of choice in the ad game.

Now that part is definitely right on: advertising and alcohol went hand in hand.

Take the case of my pal Jim Beardsley…

The cab-driving copywriter… never missed a lunch he couldn't drink

Jim was a veteran Chicago advertising agency copywriter who, I guess, you could tab as a "journeyman" wordsmith. He labored at large and small agencies pounding out mostly mundane copy for catalogs and magazines. It was sort of boilerplate stuff but very necessary blocks of prose.

Jim, a member of our Chez Paul Restaurant lunch gang in the mid-1950's, was a character right out of "Mad Men;" hard-living and hard-partying. When in his work mode, Jim was a pretty fair copy guy. Like Jon Hamm of "Mad Men," he could drink martinis with the very best of any Madison Avenue expense account-bolstered media peddler in the ad world.

I first met Jimbo, as we called him, a Robert Redford look alike, in 1955 when I was in charge of "traffic control" at the Russell M. Seeds Ad Agency in the Palmolive Building Tower. I was to make sure the writers and artists met their deadline for Raleigh Cigarettes, Sheaffer Pens, Tide detergent and other ad accounts. More than once, I had to stand and block Jimbo's office door, refusing to let him go out for lunch until he pounded out some overdue copy. I was his resident babysitter.

Jimbo *lived* for lunch… martinis… and when I was with him at our favorite watering hole, I'd joke that we didn't need a wristwatch to tell it was high noon.

"Just listen to the ice cubes in Jimbo's vodka martini clinking in his shaking hands. Yes, it must be noon," we'd say.

After the Seeds agency, Jimbo worked in Chicago at Young & Rubicam Ad Agency on a major automobile account, General Motors. His assignments were the creation of technical brochures and newspaper ads.

Auto advertising accounts could be volatile so when car sales are in the dumpster or massive factory recalls take place, it can be rough on everyone in the car biz. If you think the cut backs affect only assembly line workers, think again. When an auto company ad account goes away or is chopped, many people working for that client can be fired.

I remember in 1969, 79 people at Chevrolet's Detroit ad agency Campbell Ewald were axed in one day because of a UAW strike. No cars produced = no advertising produced = no jobs. Jimbo got caught up in a situation like that at Young & Rubicam in the fifties and got canned.

However this was not going to affect the lifestyle of affable, outgoing James Beardsley's GQ's concept of an advertising agency playboy; handsome, rugged… a Brooks Brother's fashion plate with an engaging and blustery personality. He was still one of the "boys at the bar" and being kept from his noontime Smirnoff on the rocks and schmoozing schedule was not sitting well with Jimbo. Chez Paul Francais was his club… his hangout… his gang. He was determined that being "on the beach" and job hunting was not going to have a negative effect on his mid-day martini routine.

Jimbo's plight took a humorous turn. The ad job market situation got so bad he took a job driving a Checker Cab in downtown Chicago. He had bills to pay and a hard-drinking wife to support. Despite this new and seemingly menial occupation, driving people around Chicago's Loop to various hotels, he managed to steer near his favorite watering hole and to maintain his "adman" lifestyle with a liquid lunch each day at Chez Paul.

One bright summer day after Jimbo had parked his Checker Cab about a half-block from his favorite French watering hole, he was on his second martini when a space sales rep from *Time Magazine*, on the lookout for someone upon who he could use his generous expense account to pay for a couple lunches and martinis, spotted Jimbo.

Not knowing he was unemployed from his big ad agency General Motors ad job, the guy launched into a pitch on why Jim's client should be buying ads in *Time*. He downed the Smirnoff's and they kept coming. Jimbo let him chatter, pitch on, slurp and slurp. After all, it was a free cocktail session.

As the clock on the wall edged toward 2:00 p.m., and the bistro emptied, the *Time* sales guy asked for the tab. His new "sales prospect," Jimbo, sauntered out of the restaurant to head to work.

The *Time* sales guy caught him in the parking lot and said, "Thanks Jim. Let's talk some more about GM coming on board. Let's take a cab. Can I drop you at your office?"

Jimbo took off his Brook Brothers sport coat, reached into his Checker Cab, retrieved his peaked cabby cap and said, "Sure, let's take mine."

I was sitting in a window booth with some of our lunch group, Dudley Bowlby, Wally Dawson and bistro owner Bill Contos. We were in stitches.

When he arrived back at the *Time* rep's office, Jimbo said, "That'll be nine dollars and 40 cents before the tip." *A classic adman story.*

Pat McCormick… it was always show time!

The tallest regular on the Windy City Watering Hole Circuit was Pat McCormick. You know him as the 6' 7"comedian. I got to know him as the Parade Magazine ad salesman!

Even though his "official" bio says Pat started in the ad game in New York after a stint in the U.S Army, he was actually working in the Chicago market when I first met him. The "official" bio reads like he went into the ad game in New York, not as a lower-rung space peddler (which he was) in Chicago.

He was selling advertising space for *Parade Magazine* and I was handling the advertising for Curtiss Candy's Baby Ruth, Butterfinger and assorted brands.

I knew he was a bit on the loony side because of the first time he called on me at my office. Our receptionist announced him. As I was staring at the top of my office entrance expecting a 6' 7" giant, all of a sudden, I see this 270-pound hulk crawling into my office.

Show time!

Pat McCormick –
Writer and actor

Pat McCormick got his start in Chicago. I spent many nights with this funnyman and fellow comic Jonathan Winters at some of Chicago's favorite watering holes.

I gave him some ad business. He also was a pal of Jonnie Winters. We were all about the same age and full of energy, so we hit it off.

We socialized quite a bit and made the rounds of Chicago's watering holes. We hooked up with Winters on a couple of insane evenings of carousing.

It was hard to believe the big guy was a champion hurdler at Harvard. He was. Every place we went, McCormick brought down the house including Mr. Kelly's, other clubs on Rush Street and a couple Chicago Bears football games.

During one freezing game at Wrigley Field (the Bears played there) where I had primo 10th row seats behind the Bears dugout, Pat went out for beer and then couldn't find our seats. I looked up and he was actually standing on top of the Bears dugout facing the vast audience shouting "Maloney... where are you?"

While I was working on the prestigious American Marketing Association luncheon appearance featuring my client David Reynolds, CEO of Reynolds Metals Company, I had a series of lunch meetings with AMA Executive Secretary Dick Revnes. I brought Pat along for comic relief. He lightened up the meetings.

Revnes, another guy who was Pat's and my age, was a charismatic dynamo and was planning the first ever Chicago International Trade Festival at Navy Pier. All of Chicago's major businesses were to be represented. There were to be music, entertainers, water shows... a real gala.

Revnes thought Pat was a real hoot. Though McCormick had no on-stage experience, Dick offered him a neat spot in the festival... a paid gig. With his great humor, Pat was supposed to wander around the audience at various entertainment venues with a microphone to interview folks from all over the U.S. The on-stage host emcee was to say, "Now here's Pat McCormick... a very funny guy. Who are you with Pat?"

Pat agreed to the deal, but was apprehensive about appearing before a live audience that would also involve some TV coverage. Dick actually had to talk him into doing the gig. I was also apprehensive because Pat liked to have a few toddies before being funny.

The big day came for him to appear and Pat was a no-show. He spent the afternoon at Chez Paul. He forgot about the gig. That's when I knew he was really odd.

A couple weeks later he said, "Bill, I have an offer from Jack Parr to be one of his comedy writers but it's a four-month trial. If I quit my job, go to New York and it doesn't work out, I'm on the beach. What do you think?"

I knew he was a bit on the crazy side but extremely talented. I talked him into it and we had a big going-away party. I was even able to get the NBC chopper to take him to O'Hare Field and off to the Big Apple.

He made it with Jack Parr and later headed for Hollywood. He appeared in "Smokey and The Bandit," starred with Bill Murray and appeared in a slew of TV shows including "The Gong Show," "Bill Cosby," and "I've Got a Secret."

He wrote for those shows as well as for Jack Paar, Danny Kaye and Johnny Carson. His best pal was 5' 3" comic/songwriter Paul Williams… the original odd couple, since Pat was a 6' 7" giant.

I'll always remember the time in Chicago when four of us, Pat, his girlfriend, a date and I were moseying down Rush Street. We passed a tavern where a comely lady waved at Pat. I thought they knew each other. They did not.

Pat said, "Go ahead… I'll catch up."

He ran into the saloon. We didn't see him for three days. *True story.* I think the woman was comedian Jaye P. Morgan. He later spent time with her in Hollywood.

Ideas, ideas… Mitch Miller and "Sing Along with Mitch"

Mitch Miller – I pitched little-known summer replacement, "Sing Along With Mitch" to NBC. It became a hit and a Friday night fixture at NBC.

Ideas are the engine that drives advertising and it seemed like I was full of them. Some of them came to me and others fell into my lap.

One of the later involved Mitch Miller. I bumped into Mitch in the Pump Room of the Ambassador East Hotel in Chicago and it was a fortuitous meeting. At the time, I was with NBC and I discovered, in a veritable pile of trash, a copy of a one-hour TV show that Mitch did for NBC called "Sing Along with Mitch." It was a low budget summer replacement for some series Ford was sponsoring and NBC considered it just to be that.

A replacement. I told Mitch I thought it was great and should be a network program but my only sales tool was a kinescope of a show.

Of course, he agreed enthusiastically and went to his room at the Ambassador and brought me a 16mm version of his show.

Yes, he did. We pitched… and the rest is history. "Sing Along with Mitch" ran for five successful seasons, becoming a Friday night fixture on the NBC schedule.

Some ideas are relative… literally… "Coroner Chicago"

In Chicago, the Cook County Coroner has more law enforcement authority than the mayor. The Coroner's Office, especially in Crimeland USA, was a heavy-duty job. My uncle Walter McCarron was elected Coroner in 1952.

A little known fact is that the Coroner did not have to be a doctor or even have medical experience. In typical Chicago fashion, it's a political / management position with high media visibility.

While working at the Clinton E. Frank Ad Agency in 1959, I had an idea for a TV series centered on the Office of the Coroner of Cook County. My uncle, the Coroner of the most famous crime city in the U.S., had more files and infamous death weapons than any Coroner's Office in the country.

Chicago was always considered the crime capital of the world. It was a treasure trove of story lines, scripts and props for a TV series… just like the immensely popular weekly show, "Dragnet."

This could be money in the bank. The story lines were already created… and they were real, not fiction. I grabbed one of our copywriters Ed Jansen and paid Uncle Walter a visit at the Coroner's Office.

He showed us famous crime files and knives, pistols, shotguns, hatchets and court transcripts from hundreds hideous past Chicago land marquee big names: Al Capone, John Dillinger, Baby Face Nelson, Machine Gun Kelly, Bonnie and Clyde, Roger Touhy.

There was a treasure trove of material for a scriptwriter. The title of the program would be "Coroner Chicago." I figured that really said it all… needed no explanation.

However, writers have to be paid, marketing is expensive and I had yet to figure out how to go about selling a concept… so the idea languished.

I was a half-century ahead of "CSI!" And in advertising, not only can you be too far behind; you can be too far ahead!

A COMEDY SIDEBAR

*Anyone for a laugh? I was a total ad exec
and half a comedian.*

You can't survive in this business without a sense of humor. Usually I was behind the scenes making products and people look good, but on a few occasions, I was the center of attention. Being around truly funny guys like Jonathan Winters and Pat McCormick, you couldn't help picking up on their dialects, delivery, improv and timing.

More than once, beginning at University of Illinois, I was the guy with the lampshade on my head at parties. I thought I was funny, I was told I was funny, but it wasn't until I met Winters and McCormick did I realize I was a true amateur. Being around those guys was a humbling experience.

Here are a few of my favorites, sans Winters and McCormick...

Toni Meloni... hoodlum bill collector

I was at my desk in New York, 1964, working on annual ad budgets for my client Canadian Club. I received a call from my favorite Chicago bistro owner and pal, Bill Contos, proprietor of Chez Paul Restaurant Francais, a favorite Windy City media watering hole and Jonathan Winter's favorite Chicago pit stop.

Bill said, "Willy (how we addressed each other), I had a big shot businessman in my restaurant several weeks ago who entertained a dozen people for dinner. *Big tab*. He was going to pay with American Express, but since he looked very prosperous to me, I told him I could bill him directly to his office in New York. I've billed him... no pay. I called him and he said he'd pay immediately. That was three weeks ago. Got any ideas how I can get this clown to pay up?"

I got the guy's phone number from Bill. I called him.

In my best Chicago thug accent said, "Mr. Smith... my name is Tony Meloni. I'm downstairs in your building. I collect debts and I have one here from Shez (not Chez) Paul in Chicago and I want to collect... or... or... "Smith" is all flustered since obviously I sounded Mafioso.

He said, "I'll pay it immediately."

I shot back, "You'd better... or else."

Two weeks go by and Mr. "Smith" hasn't paid. Bill called me again.
I told Bill I'd go after the guy. I called "Smith" and in my best George
Raft impersonation, I told him I was on my way up the elevator to
"collect"... whereupon he said, "Stop. I'll pay it right now!"

An hour later Bill Contos calls me from Chicago and says he just
received his money via Western Union. We both had a good laugh.

My short acting career... as an Italian

My improv began suddenly in college. One of the guys in the frat
house at University of Illinois was Tony Delvecchio, a big guy and
clone of movie star Victor Mature. He was a theater major. All Tony
wanted to do was be an actor. He talked about it constantly.
He dreamt about being on stage.

He took acting lessons and auditioned for anything that came along
in local theater. Personally, I didn't think he was very good but he
worked hard, rehearsed and kept persevering towards a career
on the stage. Tony told me about a new production in the works
on campus; a big show.

He said they needed extras and second bananas. He kept asking me,
"Why don't you go over to The Illini Theatre Group and audition?"

I told Tony that I had no desire to act, and I'd be petrified in front of
an audience even though he knew that when I had a couple of beers
in me I was the town clown.

He kept pushing until I said, "Okay, I'll sign up for a quickie audition."

The big day came and I fortified myself with three beers before
my big debut.

The director said, "This is an improv thing. We want to look you over.
Pretend you just got off a boat from Europe and there is nobody
here to meet you at the dock and you don't know what to do."

Out of the blue I launched into an Italian dialect, "My name… is… my… name is Giuseppe Farina… I… I… I do no how to speak English. I'm-a simple cabinet maker from Modena… my cousin Luigi said he would be here at the dock… I'm-a confused… maybe I want to go back… (cry) where are you Luigi????"

I played the lost soul looking for my cousin and not finding him on the dock. I recalled my hard life in Italy and broke down crying… "I have a-no money I have no telephone number… what will I do???"

There was no audience in the empty theater so it was fun.

Three days later I received a call at the frat house from the Illini Theatre Group director saying they wanted me in the show! **Me?** A neophyte, *first timer*. I was in shock.

Then a letter came to the frat house for Tony, the dedicated student actor. The show director said, "Sorry, you didn't make it. We have no room for you in the show." He was devastated.

I felt sorry for him, and no, I've never seen his name on any movie or TV show credits.

As for my theatre career and me, I never even responded to the director… never went out for the part. It was a lark. I had no plans to be an actor.

Jerry Lewis… I was his doppelganger

It was in a Milwaukee saloon with a group of ad exec buddies when I gave what was perhaps my finest acting performance, surpassing even my University of Illinois drama club tryout. And it was all an accident.

For many years, starting with their appearances on the Ed Sullivan show, Jerry Lewis and Dean Martin were my favorites. I followed all the performances and I even rehearsed a mini Jerry Lewis take-off I would do for friends.

Eventually, Lewis started taking himself too seriously as a movie star and he split with the Martin. He also started his Jerry's Kids Labor Day Muscular Dystrophy charity drive, certainly a worthwhile charity, but he wasn't funny anymore. I became disenchanted with the guy.

However there is an odd twist. In the late 1950's I went through a stage where I closely resembled Jerry Lewis. Occasionally people would point this out to me. *Kind of weird.*

I was in Milwaukee, 1959, to work on some TV commercials for Fort Howard Paper Company, a huge manufacturer in Green Bay that made a hundred types of industrial and institutional paper towels and napkins. They wanted my agency to take them retail. We designed the line, named it Petal Soft, and were kicking off with TV spots in Milwaukee as a test market. I was to go to the local NBC station to make sure our new commercials were aired correctly.

With a few hours to kill, I met two media salesman friends of mine; Dudley Bowlby, *Time Magazine*, and Jeff Martini from *U.S. News & World Report* for a couple of beers. Jerry Lewis was in town to premiere his new movie, "Geisha Boy," and had just conducted a press conference in this restaurant. He had just walked out and we walked in.

Two guys at the bar waived to the three of us and said, "Hey Jerry! Glad you came back. We love you."

Interesting, I thought. What's brewing? Obviously these two guys, rich homebuilders with matching Cadillacs in the parking lot, had been boozing in this joint most of the day.

They sent down drinks to us and said, "Hey Jerry, you're great."

They kept calling me Jerry. My two pals loved it… *free drinks.* I told the two contractors I wasn't Jerry Lewis.

Jerry and his doppelganger, me!

"In fact," I said, "look at the inside of my coat pocket with a Chicago department store label. Sure, sure Jerry, you want to be private," they said, refusing to believe I wasn't Lewis.

After a couple beers, I went to the men's room; I came out feeling frisky and like an idiot. I did my Jerry Lewis routine.

"Hey, Dino, I didn't do it... hey, Dino," I wailed with my hair askew and stumbling knock-kneed. Crazy... crazy. The two guys were then convinced that I was the real deal.

Jack Teagarden, "Father of Jazz Trombone" and his band were headlining at the Brass Rail Club just down the block from our saloon. These two guys insisted I should meet him. I said "no." My buddies insisted and all of them proceeded to drag me out the door and down the street to The Brass Rail... and Teagarden...
me protesting all the way.

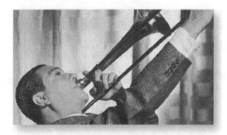

Jack Teagarden goes along with my gag!

We're in Milwaukee and, as usual, it was ten below zero and snowing.

Teagarden is on stage... the place is jumping... he says,
"Hi Jerry... welcome!"

I did a quick flustered explanation telling him that I wasn't Jerry Lewis.

"It's a gag. These guys are crazy," I nervously explained.
"My pals are having fun."

He said, "I understand. I'll fix it. Have a seat..."

Suddenly, there's a very pretty young lady seated next to me and she says, "Are you really Jerry Lewis?"

"Sure I am!"

CHAPTER SIX

Fun, sad and mad ad tales from Chi town

Here's a collection of memorable people and experiences I had while in the game. I guess I could write some scholarly theories of marketing and advertising here… but who wants to read that? I think anyone reading this book will want to read about people and how the admen and women (both the advertisers and their clients) make it work… or not work. Success in advertising takes some intelligence, some guts and a whole hell of a lot of luck… like being in the right place at the right time… or how a near disaster can end up to be a big win… and dealing with smooth talkers. My war cry has always been, "TIMING AND DELIVERY."

The admen salesmen… winding up for the pitch

As illustrated in AMC's Emmy-winning "Mad Men" TV series set in the 1960's, the mid–1950 were also a very competitive time. Big agencies with the proper resources could hire full time new business executives carrying the title "New Business Development Director." These guys who had business or old school connections belonged to the *right* country clubs and could get in the door to set up pitches to major ad prospects.

It was a perilous job as the new business dude had just one function: **sell** not **create** good advertising or even service client accounts. They were told to *"Get our shop in the door and get an appointment for a formal business presentation!"* In most cases that was their sole assignment.

At Clinton E. Frank Advertising we had a couple of real hot shot new "business guys," Perry Brand and Bowman "Bo" Kreer. These two men had a pretty good track record for signing on new business. And they were expensive.

They offered their expertise to ad agencies as a team. They rehearsed and had scripted lines. They were all show biz. They'd kickoff their spiel by showcasing their personal and business credits to the point of making the audience feel they were in the presence of greatness.

Bo Kreer would say, "Perry, my associate was a U.S. Army medal award ace fighter pilot. He was the highest grossing sales guy at *This Week Magazine;* $15 million in ad sales."

Perry Brand would follow with, "Aw shucks, Bo. Knock that off. Did you all know that Bo wrote the best selling marketing book that is a staple in advertising classes at major colleges and universities including Northwestern?"

Their two-man road show would knock the socks off most people in the room. They were impressive and most of the time their spin worked. We, the guys on the firing line, knew they were professional BS artists but at least they were *our* BS artists. I often wondered if the business they acquired actually paid for the cost of their services.

Brand finally got canned by Clint Frank for "breaking some company accounting rules." Bo finally got tired of Perry's questionable practices. He quit the ad game and became a marketing instructor at Loyola University.

Ripping up the Baby Ruth board room

This one was a real goof-up. After several preliminary presentations where we beat out seven big Chicago ad agencies for the $1 million Curtiss Candy (Baby Ruth, Butterfinger) ad account, we were invited to the final round. It was D-Day and we were up against two major Chicago shops.

At the Curtiss Candy headquarters boardroom just down the block from Wrigley Field, we unveiled our "secret weapon;" 19 huge six-foot mounted photos depicting how we would service the prominent confectionery ad account.

This impressive display showcased our Art Department, TV Production crew, focus groups and brainstorming sessions with 30 experts.

I was depicted interviewing kids at department stores and schools asking them their candy preferences. Tongue in check, we even showed our staff boarding a yacht implying as our link to overseas markets that got a laugh.

In our zeal to present our "secret weapon," we taped all the huge photos to the client's oak paneled conference room wall. We covered each one with a nice clean white sheet. In a dramatic flourish, we ripped the sheets off the photos as we presented.

Suddenly… to our dismay we found that it was not an oak wall but instead was oak-like wallpaper. As we ripped and presented, we destroyed the room sending the wallpaper flying. Fortunately, the Curtiss execs had a sense of humor and our pitch was strong enough that we got the account.

A close call.

Combat pay for a Borg Warner ad pitch

We were going after the Borg Warner advertising account, a 75 year-old producer of a great many components for automobiles, including manual and automatic transmissions, and a leading supplier to **all** the auto companies.

Though an industrial account wasn't worth a bunch of money it was a prestigious piece of business that could very well attract more Midwestern old-line companies.

The hard-drinking advertising manager's daddy, Ray Ingersol was the Borg Warner CEO. The poor kid, who was constantly wooed by Chicago ad agencies, was a complete dunce. He had no clue what his job entailed and his office was one huge pile of files and ancient correspondence.

My boss, Clint Frank said, "We're sure we want their account but I'm not having lunch with that boozer. Nobody can keep up with his martini drinking. So, Bill; it's your turn in the barrel. Go meet the guy. *We'll give you combat pay.*"

So I made the lunch date. With this dude it was always lunch. We went to my favorite watering hole, Chez Paul. Since I knew Benny the bartender (I had hired him to play a real live gaucho in a Tango candy bar TV commercial) I told him the clown with me would drink vodka martinis but to give me water on the rocks with an olive.

Six martinis (for him) later and no lunch, I put the guy in a cab and he went home. That's the end of the Borg Warner new business possibility. Good riddance.

No, there was no combat pay… just a slap on the back for taking one for the team.

The Green Bay Packers came calling

One day the Green Bay Packers came calling at the Clinton E. Frank Agency. They needed to hook up with an advertising or PR agency to help them with television network negotiations and possibly even TV commercial production. I was the TV guru at the agency, involved with the spooky show-biz world of network television. I practically lived at 30 Rockefeller Center, 20 weekends a year.

One of my advertising account responsibilities was to service the Fort Howard Paper Company in Green Bay, Wisconsin. I was in and out of Green Bay four times per month. I arranged for Fort Howard to co-sponsor the television kickoff of the Packers new stadium Lambeau Field. So I knew my way around Green Bay.

Vice President Richard Nixon flew in for the event.

The real reason that the Packers came to us for television counseling was not that I knew Green Bay or the TV industry. It was because the main man at our agency, Clint Frank, was football's Heisman Trophy winner and was spending $10 million per year for our clients in network television.

Dominick Olejniczak, president of the Packers, called and asked if we would come to Green Bay to meet with him and some of his people on the upcoming negotiations with major television networks for Packer football game telecasts. This, of course, was before the NFL took over TV responsibilities. Clint was scheduled to go to Europe and asked me to go to Green Bay and rap with Dominick and his guys to see what they had in mind. They really didn't seem to have a handle on the situation and we weren't too positive about what we could do for them, but it sure would've been a gold star to have the world champion Green Bay Packers on our client list.

In the Packer's reception lobby waiting for a lunch meeting with Olejniczak, I saw a halfback from Purdue get his walking papers. He was told he was cut. It was very emotional, as he sobbed to everyone in the room. He had just moved his family to Green Bay, bought a house and now he's out of work. This was clearly the downside of the pros.

Dominic and I talked for a couple of hours but nothing concrete came out of the discussion as we really didn't know the numbers coming from the networks or what other teams were doing TV wise. It really wasn't an ad agency gig.

As I look back on a possible missed opportunity, I can't help but think of how much fun it would've been to be tied in with one of the great NFL football teams.

More fun times in Green Bay… and a possible disaster

At Clinton E. Frank Advertising, one of our clients was Fort Howard Paper Company in Green Bay. Chances are that when you stop for a hamburger today you'll get it in some kind of napkin made by Fort Howard. It was a huge company down the road from Kimberly Clark.

At the agency in Chicago's Merchandise Mart, we worked for weeks on the client's annual ad campaign; consumer products, institutional, industrial. We had 40 layouts and a huge big media program.

The day before the *big* meeting ($700,000) in Green Bay we had a run through with all departments to polish the pitch. I was the account executive. We made several changes to the artwork in a dozen layouts.

We told the art director to make the changes and that he would have to work all night to get it done.

The next day, Clint, department heads and I took he company plane to Green Bay. I laid out everything out in the Fort Howard conference room. To my horror, I found *all* of the revised layouts were missing.

The art director said, *"I thought **you** were bringing them."* His assistant said, *"I thought **you** were bringing them."* It's zero hour and the meeting is at hand. ***Panic time!***

We called the office in Chicago, told them to run to the airport and get the layouts on a plane to Green Bay immediately. All the ads were for a Fort Howard corporate image campaign. These were *Newsweek, Time,* and *Forbes, US News & World Report* ads.

The meeting started and I do the pitch… *s l o w l y* . As we were getting closer to the image campaign, I heard an airplane overhead since the airport was nearby. I just knew it had to be our ad material. We all sensed it and we all started vamping… *BS-ing… dragging on the presentation… waiting for the package… bad jokes… how are your kids… what will the Packers do this year… and it went on and on.*

It did arrive about 20 minutes later. We finished the presentation, *wowed* the executives and got the program approved.

Whew! Close call. I was running out of Jonathan Winters routines.

My "dream vacation" to outer space

Keeping with the idea of continuous entertaining in the ad world, Clint Frank threw a costume party for ad executives and clients at his beautiful mansion in the northern suburbs of Chicago. It was complete with prizes for costumes based on the "Vacation We'd Like to Take." Most of the *non-creative* types came in their ski clothes or golfing duds.

At the time, I was commuting weekends to NBC in New York, so I had access to one of the largest costume departments in the U.S. I picked out two costumes from the "Tom Corbett Space Cadet" TV show for myself and a date. The concept was: *a vacation in space*. It was a weird costume and despite a bunch of Canadian Club, I still couldn't fly.

Thought for sure I had won the thing until a pal of mine, copywriter Roy Lang, who had some kind of ties to the Chicago Stadium, arrived with a huge bathrobe with his name on the back ("10-second Lang"), boxing trunks, headgear, black eye and boxing gloves. His favorite vacation was his training camp in the Catskills, which was where most boxers trained. He got me.

I am "Captain Wonderful" and my "dream vacation" is outer space. Borrowed from the NBC New York Costume Shop ("Tom Corbett Space Cadet Show"), I thought I won the big Clint Frank costume party, but I didn't. A copywriter beat me with an even better costume.

Helping out a frat brother

It's always been a great feeling to help out somebody through connections. This is one of my favorites.

One of my fraternity brothers at University of Illinois was Illini quarterback Don Engles. A big, strong guy from the prestigious high school, St. George in Evanston, Illinois. St. George was a powerhouse in football, winning the 1943 and 1953 City Bowl. Don alternated at quarterback with Tommy O'Connel. He threw a 60 yard touchdown in the '52 Rose Bowl.

When he got out of school, he went to the Chicago Cardinals. He was injured and went to play in Canada where he was hurt again.

I bumped into him late one night on Rush Street. He was in the dumps thinking since he couldn't play football… now what?

I got him an interview with Harry Pucetti, CEO of Hornblower & Weeks Stockbrokers. I told Harry that though Donnie Boy was a jock he was a *quarterback* and those guys were supposed to have some smarts.

He was hired and did well. I'll never forget the time at the Chicago Athletic Club when I fixed Engles up with a date, my sister Patsy. Don's boss, Pucetti, was at an adjoining table with his No.1 client. I sensed he'd ask Don to come over and meet the guy. He did. I said "Don, shine that Rose Bowl ring on that guy."

Next thing I see is Pucetti looking well pleased as Don diagrammed his touchdown Rose Bowl play for the client." ***I told you so.***

Engles went on to make a ton of money.

How about Motorcycle advertising with Honda?

Lots of *crotch rockets* are sold each year. Fifty thousand bikers converge on Sturgis, South Dakota annually for the world's largest "bike-in" and most are Harley Davidson's.

Harley, U.S. made, Indian and British bikes owned the motorcycle sales market for decades. Harley's were big, powerful, and noisy. Their owners were usually clad in leather because if you went down and crashed, leather kept you from getting cut up. Leather seemed to define the Harley rider… created a macho persona… tough guy genre. It was not a very attractive image. Motorcycling since its inception was a somewhat off beat, non-mainstream automotive sports activity sometimes associated with bike clubs and gangs until 1962.

Then along came Honda… Mr. Soichiro Honda was a motor head, mechanic, visionary, and racer who maintained "there must be a better way" so he created a line of sport cycles that were as powerful as Harley Davidson's but weighed one-third less, were quiet, priced for anyone who desired two-wheel transpo to work or weekend touring. Mr. Honda struck gold when his ad agency, Grey Advertising, New York created a campaign built around the headline, *"You Meet the Nicest People on a Honda!"*

Suddenly the world of motorcycling was turned upside down. Anyone could ride a Honda and have an enjoyable time. This theme ushered in the cycling "Harris Tweed" set… the "Tam & Tassel" gang. Gentleman's weekend touring clubs sprouted up everywhere.

It was a fantastic boost to the motorcycle industry. Cycling activity… lightweight two wheelers that could be ridden by women… with husbands… boyfriends. Motorcycle fun days were here. I definitely think Honda's ad slogan was responsible for expanding the industry and motorcycling acceptance.

I handled the advertising for the Honda Motorcycle dealers in six Midwestern states in 1963-64. The client gave me a small one to play with… a CT70 Mini Trail Bike. It was a blast. I could ride the thing in through the front door of Hobson's Saloon on State Street, Chicago… terrify the entire bar patrons and drive it right out the back door.

That is until Homer Hobson put it in his storeroom and told me it had been stolen. But that's a story for another day.

To offset the motorcycle buyer's misconception that a bright orange seemingly delicate appearing Honda 1200 bike was not as rugged as a big brutish Harley, I gave one to Chicago Bears all-star linebacker George Connor. At 6'4" 260 pounds, a product of Notre Dame and the U.S. Navy (and his model wife) he was also a popular Chicago figure.

Connor appeared in our TV commercials and newspaper ads. Obviously, if one of the most rugged athletes in the world chose a Honda it must be good. Though I have to admit he looked a little overpowering on the bike.

To celebrate a record sales event, Mr. Soichiro Honda visited Chicago and I arranged a reception for him at the Drake Hotel.

The highlight of the soiree was a full size ice carving of a Honda 1500 and Mr. H was thrilled.

George Conner attended and everyone was happy.

I invented party history at Northwestern football games:

TAILGATING!

And then there are the ideas that you can't copyright or trademark. You just have them and unleash them.

Tailgating at sporting events probably goes back to when Kirk Douglas was battling fellow Gladiator Russell Crowe at the Coliseum while the locals feasted on mutton and mead in the chariot parking area. But as far as who started the crazy outdoor party at Northwestern games in Evanston, it was yours truly.

Because my boss, former Heisman winner Clint Frank was on the Board of Trustees at Northwestern, I made all their games, and I'm absolutely positive we inaugurated, kicked off and started the tailgating tradition at Northwestern.

Dyche Stadium at Northwestern University was the scene for tailgating.
I take full credit for starting the tailgating tradition at NU games. Beginning
with McDonald's hamburgers from the first store in Des Plaines,
we soon graduated to full bars and a huge buffet.

In 1955, we thought it might be a cool idea to stave off the crowds, get a good parking space at Dyche (now Ryan Field) Stadium by bringing a couple sandwiches, cokes and arrive at parking an hour early.

That was neat so the next week we took burgers from the new Des Plaines McDonald's that opened in the spring and got great close-up parking.

This idea escalated to where we then made hot food, brought a few beers and had a pre-game party. Nobody else was doing this... but it started to catch on.

This went on and on every week and escalated to a point, 50 games later, where we stocked up three station wagons parked side by side and we now went to the stadium two hours prior to kick off.

Wagon No. 1
Had the bar; a real bar with hot toddies for the game.

Wagon No. 2
Had hors oeuvres; crackers, cheese, celery, shrimp (always shrimp) and assorted snacks.

Wagon No. 3
Had the food; mostaccioli, fried chicken, hamburgers.

Folding tables and chairs were set up; a record machine (yes, "record machine") played all the Big Ten fight songs ("On Wisconsin," "Go You Northwestern").

We would feed the parking attendants every week so they began roping off our tailgating
space in the most desirable front row section of the nearest parking lot to our seats.

People came from all over to see what the loonies in purple were doing party-wise this week.

And as we were smack in front of the main entrance/parking lot to our grandstand we'd greet and sometimes entertain dozens of "friends" each home game weekend. It got to be a time consuming weekly project.

Many phone calls on who brings what... the timetable... guests we may expect... meeting points and constant massaging the big party plan which almost became more important than who NU was playing.

And it all started with a McDonald's cheeseburgers and fries.

And... as they say... "the rest is party history."

CHAPTER SEVEN

The Big Apple beckons... but it's back to Chicago!

My very best Chicago friend was Jim Troy who lived in Northbrook and was a production executive at NBC Chicago in the Merchandise Mart, a few floors below my Clinton E. Frank office. Like me, he was a car nut and was in the broadcasting business. We'd meet for lunch at the M&M Club (Merchants & Manufacturers) in the Mart where you are greeted by a plaque that states *Caveat Emptor* ("Buyer Beware") as you use your special card for the private club.

Because of my work on Reynolds Metals NBC TV Network activity I was ostensibly a client of his. This was a logical excuse to put me on his entertainment expense account and we also attended some motorsports events in the Midwest and in Sebring, Florida where we both assisted a fledgling radio reporter, Austin Healey enthusiast Walter Cronkite, as "spotters" for the annual 12 hour sports car race broadcast.

Jim was an Ivy Leaguer, Williams and Dartmouth. Jim's family was well heeled and I'll never forget the day he took me to the Merchandise Mart parking garage and unveiled his brand new sports car, the very first, very rare Mercedes Benz 300-SL Gull wing sports car ever seen in the Midwest. This was one of the most expensive automobiles of its time with a price tag of $7,000. A new Buick then cost about $3,500. Today these collectable go for close to $1 million at auction.

That's me test-driving (ha!) an Allard during my stint in Manhattan.

With his new inheritance (Packard Motor Company) Jim decided to dump his "salaried" NBC job and head for New York, the capital of U.S. television broadcasting to start his own program development company.

Jim's Manhattan "crash pad"

He bought a fine house in the "toney" town of Westport, Connecticut and also purchased a "crash pad" in Manhattan… good for those snowed in nights or a haven for visiting pals.

We kept in touch and as my days with the unpredictable Perry Brand at Clinton E. Frank ad agency were getting untenable, I considered looking at opportunities in the ad capital of the world… New York City.

Canadian Club and a cool apartment

I was able to take advantage of the use of Jim's apartment in the high rent district off Fifth Avenue while I went on interviews. Eventually, I landed at the ad agency for Hiram Walker as the account executive for Canadian Club Whisky and *Family Circle* magazine.

I shared a huge two bedroom apartment not far from my Madison Avenue office and adjacent to ritzy Sutton Place Co-ops where I could view Ginger Rogers practicing at the Town Tennis Club.

I shared the pad with one of Jonathan Winters pals, comedy writer, Jim Lehner, a guy I seldom saw. His day began no earlier than 6:00 p.m. as he did his pub crawling routine with fellow comedy writers. He was a funny dude.

I became "**Redline Muldoon**"

I'd meet my pal Jim Troy at a popular media type hangout, The Rose Restaurant on West 52nd Street, and that's where I got the moniker I used in many racing stories and on my race car… "Redline Muldoon."

It happened like this: After a weekend racing my Austin Healey at Limerock, Connecticut or Bridgehampton, New York or Marlboro, Maryland, where I invariably blew an engine or crashed, I'd head for Rose's and my ad gang for lunch and lies.

Jim and the guys got to calling me Muldoon so when I related my weekend race motor blast Jim would say" "Don't you ever watch your tach... *the redline...* Muldoon?" And it stuck.

I **was** "Redline Muldoon."

Lunch at The Rose and cocktails at Toots Shor's

Our evening watering hole was Toots Shor's celeb hangout on West 52nd street. That's where you'd see Jonnie Winters, Jackie Gleason and other show biz types trying to top each other gag-wise. It was always fun to see Winters.

Pat Harrington Jr. was a TV time salesman for NBC at that time. He hung out in Toot's joint and was a very funny guy. That's where he was discovered and went on to star as Schneider on the "One Day at a Time," the 70's network TV sitcom.

I rapped with Ernie Kovac's talented wife Edie Adams and she was as funny as Ernie. I could see where they'd hit it off.

Time to go home

New York was not "the city of big shoulders" and friendliness. This was cut throat... no fun. The people were surly, I never figured out the subway, it was hard to make friends because everyone went home to the suburbs at nights and weekends, and I lived in the high rent district, Park Avenue.

Commuting every few weeks to Gotham as I did in the late 1950's to work on network television programs, staying at the finest Park Avenue hotels, carrying a pocketful of company expense account cash like a rich tourist was a far cry from actually working and living there.

As I mentioned several times in these chapters, the ad game can be very satisfying. On the other hand, because of the vagaries of clients and agency relations it can also be very volatile. When an ad shop loses a major client, staffers can be terminated.

No billings/revenue = no salaries.

My New York agency lost a major account and 14 employees including me, were let go. In many cases the job terminations can be dictated by the tenure of the employee. Obviously the last ones hired are the first to be let go.

I was not overly upset being "on the street" as I was beginning to dislike living and working in Manhattan. It had a non-permanent feeling. High prices, no parking, no neighbors to fraternize with, and a general wariness and mistrust of *New Yorkers* per se had me thinking I'd better return to my roots and friends.

Madison Avenue was not the Magnificent Mile. Sure, New York is the center of commerce and culture, but, unlike Chicago, they don't lighten up. We took the ad business very seriously in the Windy City, but we also knew how to have a good time.

Thanks, but I'll take Chicago!

The Windy City as it looks today from the Chicago River.

CHAPTER EIGHT

Racing for answers… "race on Sunday, sell on Monday"

The concept of using high performance auto activity in auto ads may have emanated with Henry Ford II's theory, "Race on Sunday, sell on Monday."

Though I'd always been interested in cars, I didn't get seriously involved in car racing until I began to represent clients in the automotive field. That's when I discovered it enhanced my client relations… and it was tax deductible!

I learned that in advertising you have to practice what you preach.

And that's how I came to race sports cars!

While many businessmen get their relaxation and do their client schmoozing on the golf course, tennis court or posh clubs and restaurants, there are those of us involved in the automotive biz who spend weekends enhancing our product credibility by going out and racing the darn things… ala Roger Penske and engineers and executives at major auto makers.

Most of the automotive accounts I managed had some sort of motorsports program; Porsche, Chevrolet, Austin Healey, MG, Pontiac, Dodge division of Chrysler Corporation.

Many of us who were inept at tennis, golf and poker but possessed a competitive urge and would spend our weekends at some out-of-the-way down and dirty racetrack miles from home banging gears and losing sleep.

My rationale for spending all of my free hours in a filthy auto garage, tuning carburetors, rebuilding motors, overhauling gearboxes, stringing wire wheels, wiring car trailers and then hauling the racer 200 miles to a racing venue was, as I said in one of my ads, "Racing For Answers."

(At least that's the way I explained this expenditure to the IRS.)

The tach's the limit… no physical restrictions in auto racing

I was always a bit on the small side… lightweight in baseball, football and basketball. In auto racing, there are no restrictions on size except the size of your *cojones*.

The basic tools you need to race successfully are skill and spunk.

In my 15 years of automotive competition, I raced Austin Healey 3000, formula Vee, Elva Courier, Triumph Spitfire, Porsche 356, and Corvette. And in the latter days of vintage racing Jaguar X K120 MC and Austin Healey 100M.

From dirt tracks to Daytona to Jay Leno's garage…
I raced 'em

My last race car, Austin Healey 100M, is in Jay Leno's Big Dog Garage, Burbank, California.

This expensive hobby took me to racetracks all over the United States, including Upper Marlboro in Maryland; Connellsville in Pennsylvania; Wilmot Hills, Black-Hawk Farms, Milwaukee Fairgrounds, Road America and Lyndale Farms in Wisconsin; Indianapolis Raceway Park in Indiana; Grand Rapids, Grayling, Detroit and Michigan International Speedway in Michigan; Donneybrooke in Minnesota; Mid-Ohio Sports Car Course in Ohio; Thompson and Lime Rock in Connecticut; Bridgehampton in New York; Gateway Raceway in Missouri; Meadowdale Raceway Lawrenceville in Illinois; Laguna Seca, Willow Springs and Infineon, in California; Jensen in Iowa; and the big one: Daytona International Raceway, Florida.

It was heady stuff; that is, if you were super serious about taking home the gold. I got the racing bug while at NBC watching a co-worker friend of mine, Tom Petri, race his Alfa Romeo on a one-mile road course in Wilmot Hills, Wisconsin.

I was hooked and thought, "If Tom can do it, I can do it."

So I embarked on a serious motorsports odyssey that was expensive, enlightening and sometimes rewarding.

ROAD AMERICA, ELKHART LAKE, WISCONSIN, 1966 --
Victorious in a monsoon at #1 position lapping 29 cars including second place Triumph of John Weinberger as I win the Badger 200.

Along the way, I won the grueling Badger 200 mile Race at Road America Elkhart Lake, Wisconsin in a pitch-dark monsoon and besting 41 other racers.

I qualified and competed in the American Road Race of Champions (ARRC) at the fabled high-banked Daytona International Speedway. I burst a tire in the third lap but was able to repair the damage and finish the race as seventh in class; that is seventh in the U.S. It was a sizzling 120 degrees on the racetrack.

One of my mechanic helpers, Steve Carmick, spent the night partying three hours away in Ft. Lauderdale. I was all over him for not being there on time and being ready to roll.

After the race, I pulled into the pits and a mechanic from another team said, "You got a crew guy in a cowboy hat?" I nodded yes and he said, "They just took him to the hospital."

I thought to myself, "Good. That will show him to pay attention to the team!"

The heat at the track got to him as he went to the hospital with heat prostration. **Yes,** speed costs money.

Memorable Road America...
Elkhart Lake Racing and a hot Vette

The high points of my sports car racing memories were:

1. Competing in the Olympics of Sports Car Racing, Daytona Beach, Florida;

2. Winning the Badger 200 in 1966 in a downpour, the next best race weekend was when I raced two cars in one long distance race at Elkhart Lake.

Sports Car Club of America (SCCA) racing for us amateurs consisted of two tiers: 1. Regional races usually held at small race venues; 2. National races that reward points towards a national class championship usually culminating with the run-offs during a championship race weekend at a major race track like Riverside Raceway, Daytona International Raceway, Mid-Ohio Sports Car course or Road Atlanta.

In order to qualify to compete in a national race such as the Badger 200 at Road America, you have to have three regional races on your resume. It was fall 1966 and entry blanks went out for Elkhart Lake Road America Badger 200, a 200-mile race on the four-mile, twisting 14-turn road racing course. Two drivers were mandatory since this was considered a long distance race. I entered my Healey 3000 in the D-Production category.

Then I receive a phone call from a guy named Dave Hinson, a young well-off aspiring race driver. He wanted to run his full-race Corvette in the Badger 200 but he didn't have the required three regional races completed. He knew I had a bit of political pull (my Chicago TV show) and asked if I could get him okayed to file an entry with a waiver to run in the B production class for 170 mph Corvettes.

His car was prepared by Terro Corvette in Chicago and was a sample of what serious race drivers do in order to start a competition career. Terro takes the car right off the Chevrolet assembly line and disassembles it, turning it into a full-blown race car.
Bring your checkbook.

I'd never driven a hot Corvette; that is, one that was prepared as a full-blown race car… 400 horsepower to my Healy's 215 ponies. And I yearned to try it out.

I told Dave I'd see if I could get him an entry if he OK'd me to co-drive the car with him at Road America. He agreed. I pulled it off and I got Tom Hickey to co-drive my Healey with me.

Michigan International Speedway

MICHIGAN INTERNATIONAL SPEEDWAY, IRISH HILLS, 1971 – *I am racing in my embarrassingly slow right hand drive Austin Healey 3000.*

I told Dave, a rank amateur who had never competed on a big race track and had only two regional races (I had about 40 races at his juncture) that I'd qualify the Vette for him and he could start the race.

I would actually start the race in my Austin Healey and at a prearranged point, about halfway I'd come in, hand my car over to Tom Hickey and take over Dave's Vette.

Invariably, the Badger 200 attracted a full field of over 55 race cars from A-Production Cobras, B-Production Corvettes down to Porsche, Lotus, Healey, Morgan, and Alfa Romeo.

I had a blast in qualifying. This car was a *real* race car and I was put in third place, second row pole out of 55 cars. Dave was shaking in his boots. His first big time race and he's surrounded by Cobras and hot cars from all over the Midwest. He was in the lion's den. I started my Healey in 19th position.

At the start the petrified Dave lost a dozen positions to the seasoned drivers but he soldiered on attempting to keep out of trouble. My Healey threw a timing chain in the 16th lap and I was out and waiting to take over from Dave.

He came in to the pits in an inauspicious 20th place. I took over and went Cobra hunting. I picked off several cars but couldn't regain the upfront position I had gifted Dave with and we finished somewhere in the top ten.

The big experience that day was seeing the look of terror on the 24 year-old driver's face when I told him, "You are starting up front," … in front of 54 race cars.

Whee.

That Vette is still racing and winning in vintage sports car races!

P.S. On Elkhart. At one point, I was the track announcer at Elkhart. I raced twice a year on the track for five years… Healey's, Porches, F-Vee, and Corvettes. It was and still is the best track in the U.S; four miles and 14 turns!

Mark Donohue … I almost beat the Indy winner

In the world of motorsports, Mark Donohue was known as "Captain Nice." He was the consummate professional: buttoned up, prepared, mechanically knowledgeable, fast, friendly and one of the best race drivers of his (limited) era. He was a rarity in the "He-Man" sport of auto racing in that he was an engineering graduate from an Ivy League school, Brown University.

He raced for the most winning car owner in Indianapolis car racing history, Roger Penske and won a lot of major races worldwide and in a variety of race cars. We both attended the same racing school in Lime Rock, Connecticut. I met him briefly. He was nice but a bit dull and all business.

In my early racing days, I would normally show up at a race venue driving my Austin Healey daily driver/family car with race numbers taped on the door, fitted roll bar, couple of full gas cans, spare tires, and of course a six-pack. Donohue, on the other hand, trailered his Elva Courier modified racer behind a beat up old Chevy station wagon. When you trailer your racer, you're very serious about winning. It illustrates you've tuned your racer for the track…not for the street. Radical… and this was supposed to be amateur racing.

Donohue was dead serious… born to race. In fact, he later won the 1972 Indianapolis 500. I met him at a couple of race meets before he became famous.

In 1969, I drove my Austin Healey from New York City to the Marlboro, Maryland Sports Car Track outside of Annapolis and Washington, D. C. I had never seen the place before. It was only my third real race and the East Coast competition in my class was ferocious… very serious stuff.

INDIANAPOLIS RACEWAY PARK, INDIANA, 1966 – With three Big Healeys
at full chat, I attempt an inside pass on Alan Barker of Louisville
and Norm Perkins of South Bend.

Donohue was there with his race team and his modified race car, hell bent on winning national racing points. I thought I might have an outside chance against him and a full field of Alfa Romeos, Daimler SP250, Triumphs, MGB's, Morgan's and Lotus Super sevens since my pal Lew Draper in Chicago had just sent me a brand new set of special made Goodyear race tires that fit my car. They were prototypes. Nobody else yet had this tire and my car handled just great.

Gentlemen, "Start your engines!"

I had no pit crew with me, and no one to handle a blackboard with instructions on laps to go or race position. I put my foot on it, passed a lot of cars and soon got the impression I might be running with the lead pack, which included Donohue. There was no way to find out other than read some other drivers pit board to see what lap we were on.

Big mistake.

After about 45 minutes of hot and heavy competition, I was shown the white flag by the starter *(A waving white flag)*. **Whee...** almost home. *Not quite.*

NOTE: *In professional racing, like NASCAR, stock cars and Indy Cars, the white flag means one lap to go. However in sports car racing, the white flag means be alert there's a service vehicle on the circuit.*

The white flag could have meant that an ambulance or tow truck on the track so be alert... give it plenty of room... slow down. Since I was brand new at this race stuff and obviously hadn't thoroughly read my rulebook, I didn't realize this. I guess I didn't pay attention at driving school. So I figured I had just one lap to go and possibly would get a top three finish... maybe even win the thing. I took what I figured was my final lap past the flag stand. I didn't even look up to see if there was a checkered flag, headed to the pits and parked. Surprisingly, the race continued ... **without me.** What a dummy I was. There were two more laps to go. Later, someone told me Mark Donohue won the event.

It was embarrassing when I asked race officials what happened and they explained how I goofed up the flag recognition!

Donohue went on to do great things in auto racing but was killed in a Formula One Grand Prix race practice session in Belgium. But for the rest of my life, I could chirp, "I almost beat Indy 500 winner Mark Donohue."

A sidebar… the miserable trip home from Maryland

I packed up all my racing junk and realized I was just about broke. At the track I had to buy spark plugs, Sunoco 110 octane race gas, food, hotel and I now I had but a dollar in my pocket. As I cruised up the New Jersey Turnpike I realized, "YIKES… I have to go through the tunnel into Manhattan. It costs $2.00… I have one dollar."

At the last oasis before the Holland Tunnel, I pulled into a Cities Service station and hoped I could hit up the gas jockey for a dollar to pay the tunnel toll.

I asked if they would cash a one dollar check. "No," was the Jersey boy's answer. "Company policy. "I said, "Let me talk to your boss." I did and he turned me down. *Jeez…* two bucks!

I pleaded. I told them to look at my $20,000 sports car and all the neat stuff on board. "No!" was still the answer.

Then I made my biggest boo-boo as I told them an absolutely true story thinking I'm certain they'll help me when they hear this tale.

"Look, guys. I'm cool. Last Sunday I had dinner in Bartlesville, Oklahoma with your company President, Frank Ireland, CEO of Cities Service. My brother Bob married the daughter of a V.P. of Philips Petroleum, Janet Riney. Mr. Ireland, friend and neighbor of the Riney's threw a huge party at his mansion in Bartlesville; a mansion with a huge five car garage," was my pathetic but true plea.

After hearing my seemingly outlandish story the Cities Service gas jockeys still said "No!" They must have thought I was some kind of screwball. They're thinking "Dinner with the President of Cities Service and he's hitting us up for a buck. *Gimme a break.*"

Finally a couple Midshipmen from Annapolis came along. They looked over my race car and all its equipment car and I said, "Will you give me a dollar if I give you a check for $5?" *They did.*

I went back to the Big Apple through the tunnel, wiser in several ways: make sure in the future that I have mad money and don't tell highbrow stories to the wrong people.

Ed "20 Grand" Steinbach

Though Ed was not a nationwide celebrity he was very prominent in the local Midwestern auto-racing scene. I mention him as I think he allowed me to create a "first;" a racetrack public address announcing, road racing style delivery.

Ed was the public address announcer at the quarter-mile dirt tracks that hosted midgets and stock car racing: Du Quoin Speedway, Du Quoin, Illinois; Milwaukee Wisconsin Fairgrounds; Mazon, Illinois Speed Bowl; Rockford, Illinois Speedway and Santa Fe, Illinois Raceway. He got the name "20 Grand" at a race where a driver lost control of his race car, went over the fence, crashed, demolished his car and Ed said, "There goes another 20 Grand." So the moniker stuck with him.

When European sports car road racing came on the scene at Meadowdale International Raceway in the Chicago area and Road America in Elkhart Lake, Wisconsin, Ed was completely out of his element. These new road race circuits were two-three-four miles around with over a dozen turns.

The spectators could only see small sections of the track. All Ed knew were the stock cars and midget racers and their drivers, "Red car passing the blue car and 27 was overtaking 31 and 19 is coming in the pits." Ho-hum. That bored the sports car racing spectators who would lose sight of the race pack for what seemed minutes. They had no information as to who was leading, who was crashing, what was going on.

My announcing career

By 1966, A whole new breed of racing automobiles, mostly from Europe, were competing and Ed had no clue as to how to explain a Lola T-70, Scarab, Ferrari, Lotus, Porsche, Healey, Morgan, Alfa Romeo, Triumph, Sprite, Jaguar, Chapparal and modified Corvettes. Ed was out of his element and was not peeved when I applied to take over his announcing deals at a couple road-racing tacks. Ed was getting on in years.

Being a multi-tasker with nothing better to do than handle a full-time advertising agency job, one-hour weekly television show, writing a weekly competition press magazine (which eventually became *Auto Week* magazine) auto racing column and raising two small children, I applied for the public announcer position in several of the Midwestern road racing circuits.

The announcer was located in a pagoda on the main straight and wore a headset that connected him to all the various corner workers around the track. Now I can give the spectators what they wanted to hear such as, "Car 98 eX British Army Sgt. Ken Miles is in the 427 Shelby Cobra, Lance Reventlow of the Woolworth fortune is chauffeuring a 200 mile per hour Scarab and three-time Indy 500 winner Rodger Ward is in the Aston Martin DB and James Bond look alike machine. Oh Oh! Trouble in turn three… Johnson's Ferrari Testa Rosa is upside down; Mak Kron has snuck through the pack in his RSK Porsche and takes over third-place … Midland Texas oil tycoon Jim Hall in his one-of-a-kind automatic transmission Chevy-powered chaparral is headed for the pits."

It was what the spectators wanted to hear. I went on to handle PA chores at tracks in Michigan, Iowa, Minnesota, Illinois and Wisconsin. On several occasions at Meadowdale Raceway and Road America I would be in the announcer's booth in the pagoda and say, "Next race is for D and E Production cars under two liter displacement. That means me in my number 10 Healey so I'll hand the mic over to my associate Tom Payne while I go down, get in my race car and try not to crash."

I never had any inclination to become a professional race car driver. I didn't like oval stock car tracks or open wheel (Midgets, Sprint or Indy Cars) as I preferred to be surrounded by metal fenders.

However the promoters at Santa Fe Raceway, a quarter mile clay racetrack in the Chicago suburbs decided they would stage a "Celebrity Race" in 1965. Media and local celebs and I were invited to participate.

I did and I won.

A race awakening… Jim Ladd's fatal crash

I was really getting hooked on sports car racing big time in 1967. I wanted to make a run for a national championship in my D-Production racing class which had over 200 competitors in the U.S. I had a bit of success racing in my self-modified Austin Healey 3000. I figured that to go big time I should buy the fastest Healey in the U.S.

The car I wanted belonged to Jim Ladd of Malvern, Pennsylvania, an MG-Austin dealer who had qualified for the American Road Race of Champions (billed as "The Olympics of Sports Car Racing") at Riverside Raceway in California. I wrote Jim telling him I wanted to buy his race car after he raced at Riverside. I awaited an answer.

I was having coffee with my wife one Sunday morning haranguing her about the safety aspects of auto racing; how we have roll over bars on the cars, fireproof clothing, crash helmets, safety inspectors and why the Austin Healey was a strong, safe race car. It's built like a tank. I told her that I'm going to buy Jim Ladd's racing Healey next week when he gets back from California on the way to Pennsylvania. I showed her Ladd's letter saying he would stop in Chicago and sell me his car. **Safe… fast… winner!**

Then, on my second cup of coffee, I picked up the sports page of the Sunday Chicago Tribune and read, "Pennsylvania Driver Dies in Sports Car Race in California." *Yes, it was Jim Ladd…* I was very silent.

That's when I figured out that Austin Healey's are not bulletproof.

RIVERSIDE INTERNATIONAL RACEWAY, CALIFORNIA, 1967

I was negotiating the purchase of Jim Ladd's (Lebanon, PA) Austin Healey 3000 race car until seeing this photo of Jim's fatal crash at Riverside.

Jim is circled.

CHAPTER NINE

My own racing TV show… I'm in race and ad heaven…
and an Emmy to boot!

A lot of deals were sealed at Windy City watering holes. I was part of a gang of "ad types" who congregated in a little North State Street oyster bar called Hobson's… quaint and affordable.

One evening after my workday my world changed forever. Chuck Harrison from TV station WCIU Channel 26 gave me the low down on his station, which at the time was located in The Board of Trade Building, 26th floor in the Chicago Loop. It was a weird place for a TV station as it had minimal studio space. Out of six television stations serving Chicago, I'd rank WCIU number 10. They were in the dark ages. CIU stands for Chicago's first UHF station. Here it was 1967 and they still didn't have color, however some local moneyed guys thought it was prestigious to own a TV station especially in a major market.

Chuck had an idea for a television project. It seems MGM Hollywood approached most of the Chicago television stations to taut a new James Garner movie about exciting Formula One auto racing in Europe produced by the legendary John Frankenheimer, titled "Grand Prix." Chicago was where they were going to premiere it… in one week!

MGM wanted to run a 10-minute promo on the major Chicago TV stations. But the network affiliates wouldn't take the promo. This was before infomercials.

WCIU anticipated a nice cash purchase from an advertiser other than their usual Sam's Meat Market and used car dealers said they'd attempt to put something together.

Chuck said, "Bill, you're a race nut and you've spent a lot of time in television production. How'd you like to create a half-hour one-shot TV show about auto racing and build it around a big budget Formula One movie? Heck, you can be the on-camera host."

It sounded intriguing. There were no television shows anywhere devoted to motorsports, which was and still is the number two spectator worldwide… right behind soccer. The biggest sporting event in the world spectator-wise was the Indianapolis 500 with a grandstand holding 250,000 people. At that time there were over 40 million tickets sold to racing events in the United States annually and yet no consistent TV programs devoted to the genre.

WCIU talent fee was negligible, but the challenge was formidable. I contacted a friend of mine, Al Ross, who had done some open wheel racing in Europe somewhat similar to Formula One and asked if he'd like to rap about racing in front of a TV camera.

We dug up various props involved with motorsports such as the drivers flame proof coveralls, crash helmet, goggles, safety harnesses and pictures of race cars. We swapped race stories.

All this was built around the "Grand Prix" promo, which was one of the most exciting 10-minute race TV promos I had ever seen. Twenty nine year-old-director John Frankenheimer was a genius as he improvised never-before-seen camera shots…unique camera rigs on race cars and edit bay tricks in post-production of multi-image Cinerama action scenes.

"Motorsports International" was born…
at Chicago's smallest TV station

So we did the show, which I named "Motorsports International," and screened Garner's movie "Grand Prix." I wondered if anybody watched WCIU. However, to our delight, a huge number of Chicagoland's gearheads came out of the woodwork and tuned in. In fact, it was overwhelming.

The following day, the general manager of WCIU called me and said, "That was cool. We actually had an audience. How would you like to make a steady diet of the show and do it every week Tuesday, 8:00 p.m. primetime? You write, produce and host a weekly one-hour show (jeez, now its 60 minutes… an hour a week) and we'll provide all the production facilities. You can own the commercial availabilities. "

I went to Andy Granatelli, CEO of STP and squeezed a few bucks for the production and then added a few more sponsors such as Firestone stores, speed shops and auto customizers.

One sponsor was a brand new Chevrolet dealer in Maywood, Illinois, Celozzi Ettleson Chevrolet. They had a huge, gorgeous block long dealership on highway U.S. 45.

Problem was people could see the beautiful store from the freeway but had to drive three quarters of a mile… three turns… to get to the showroom. So I came up with a TV commercial and giant billboard concept with a headline that read, "Celozzi Ettleson Chevrolet. Hard to Find… Tough to Beat." This was 1967 and they were still using that slogan in 2000.

Our audience was growing. The show added credibility to the popularity of the sport of auto racing. An audience of others beyond motor heads got a taste of high-speed motorsports action they'd never seen before but had only read about. Names of the greats and near greats in European Grand Prix racing, NASCAR Stock cars, drag racing, Midget and Sprint car racing and the emerging wildness of off-road desert racing provided exciting TV viewing fare.

"Motorsports International" was a first in the U.S.

This was the first weekly automotive-motorsports TV show in a major market in the United States. "Motorsports International" on Chicago WCIU started the whole program segment.

NOTE: Today, The Speed Channel does car-programming 24/7 and BBC's "Top Gear" weekly show is seen in 22 countries. In the U.S., there are 37 weekly television shows about cars… racing, restoring, collecting, detailing, fixing and selling at auction.

Years later, I was talking with Robert E. Peterson, CEO of Peterson Publishing, the multizillion dollar publishing empire for magazines such as Hot Rod. He told me that in 1960 they did some videos in the alley behind KTLA in L.A. for an auto show promotion.

Joking with him, I quipped, "But that wasn't the same. It wasn't the first weekly auto show in a major market."

And he agreed.

We have a hit!

Companies from all over the U.S. that were making high performance automotive products sent their representatives and big-name race drivers to Chicago to be interviewed on "Motorsports International."

We were in demand! Race driver school boss Bob Bondurant flew in from Los Angeles to do a 20-minute gig. Jaguar, Ford, Champion Spark Plug, Firestone, spending $zillions in motorsports, finally had a media outlet to promote their involvement and superior performance capabilities.

Several years prior to my TV show, Shell Oil Company spent one million dollars on five fantastic 60-minute "History of Auto Racing" films and these proved to be one of the most popular segments of my weekly TV show. Now, instead of being viewed by 30-40 people at a local auto enthusiast monthly club meeting these colorful and well produced films were viewed by 20,000 motor heads in the Chicago area each week... *prime time.*

James Garner did a phone interview and I finally did hook up with him at a charity cocktail party in Beverly Hills a few years later. Sweden's international rally ace Eric Carlson came on the show representing SAAB. Indy and NASCAR champions such as the Unsers, Bettenhausen, "Dyno" Don Nicholson, Richard Petty, George Follmer and Jaguar's Bob Tullius all came to Chicago appear on the show.

WCIU had archaic production facilities. Luckily, I had great contacts with major oil, spark plugs, tires; auto companies who provided us with program material for my one-hour show each week and we gradually built an audience.

After several weeks on the air, it was time to hear from the audience, so we decided to take phone calls. We initiated a five second delay after some clown called in and said he couldn't get "that frozen STP crap out of its can in cold weather."

Not good... STP was our main sponsor. The delay was also helpful when my buddies called in saying, "We're at Hobson's saloon waiting for you."

Ouch!

We'd only take four or five phone calls but the phone counter said we had hundreds waiting. Jesse Owens, the great Olympian, did his live sports report show immediately following my show. Often he'd pick up his phone and the caller would ask for me instead of him.

Chicagoland gearheads turned out in huge numbers to watch my TV show on Chicago's WCIU-TV, "Motorsports International." The first weekly automotive motorsports show in a U.S. major market, 1967, was featured on the Chicago Sun-Times TV Guide cover.

Chicago Midwestern Emmy Awards…
from 0 to 60 in one year… and Sammy Davis, Jr.!

At the end of our first year on the air the Chicagoland Emmy Awards were announced and "Motorsports International" was listed as one of the seven finalists in the sports category.

A big black-tie award gala was planned at the Hilton O'Hare Inn with none other than Sammy Davis Jr. hosting with music, dancing and a crowd of 2,000 attending. WCIU being the lowest TV station on the Chicago totem pole had received no nominations for Emmys other than "Motorsports International."

In less than a year, "Motorsports International" won a Chicagoland Emmy nomination second only to the Chicago Cubs live broadcasts.

The station's management was ecstatic so they reserved a table for ten at the banquet.

They freaked out when I told them I was not going to attend. I explained that I'm not in show biz… the TV show is a hobby… I'm in the advertising agency business. *Have a nice day.*

CRASH!

Everybody at the station, all my friends, and my wife wanted to lynch me for declining. Constant badgering by all my friends went on for two weeks… *me no go!*

Finally, the afternoon of the event and after a variety of threats including divorce, *I gave in.* It was so last minute I actually had to rent a tuxedo as we drove to the Hilton. I used paper clips for cuff links.

Now everyone was happy and they were even happier when out of seven contenders "Motorsports International" took second place to Jack Brickhouse and his daily telecasts of the Chicago Cubs games. I even got my own *Chicago Sun-Times* TV Guide cover.

Sammy Davis Jr. handed me a plaque and I hear that's still on display at WCIU which is still operating on the near west side of Chicago not far from skid row… but hanging in with reruns of "I Love Lucy" and "The Rifleman."

My juggling act and 80 hour weeks

Juggling a daily 9 to 5 ad agency job with writing, producing and hosting a one-hour TV show was a helluva time consuming job.

I had the program formatted into four segments: weekend racing results, celeb interview, big time race film and coming events. As things got more hectic, advertisers came on board and audience acceptance climbed. I worked hard to put out a good product.

Each week, I would spend hours blocking out the show. Remember, this is a sideline to my real job and my racing activities. I'd collate dozens of 8x10 cardboard mounted photos (WCIU didn't have a slide machine), race results and research the background on our show's guest interview.

"Motorsports International" ran 122 straight weeks… more than two years… live from Chicago on WCIU. It seemed that every Tuesday would turn out to be Christmas, New Year's, my birthday, my kids' birthday or some other holiday. There were no days off!

Though it was a heavy grind I always considered the show as a side gig to my real job with the advertising agency that provided me with the steady paycheck. However, I gained a lot of TV production experience.

I brought in knowledgeable "co-hosts" to handle segments and give me a respite. They prepared their own scripts. It worked. Time now for 'Dyno' Don Nicholson from *Hot Rod* Magazine with the weekend drag racing results." It was one big happy family.

All good things come to an end

I was riding high with my own TV show about my favorite activity, motorsports. But I still had an unfulfilled goal: to work for an advertising agency with a major automotive account.

And that's when I got the phone call from Darcy McManus in Detroit, lead agency for Pontiac nationally.

Goodbye **"Motorsports International"...** Hello commuting back and forth to Motown.

P.S. to "Motorsports International"

WCIU tried several other guys in my job. In fact one of them called me and said. "I'm lost. How do you do a whole hour every week? How did you do that?"

I said, **"Does Macy's tell Gimbel's?"**

So after a few valiant attempts to keep the program going, the station gave it up and cancelled "Motorsports International."

I was sad to see my show sacked. But, hey, I was going to be in Motown running advertising for Dodge's high performance cars.

CHAPTER TEN

Auto Advertising in the Chicago and Detroit trenches

Darcy McManus/Detroit had the account for the Midwest Pontiac dealers, a group that included dealerships in Omaha, Milwaukee, St. Louis, Kansas City, Minneapolis - St. Paul and Oklahoma City. When they called asking if I'd like to be lead account executive or the group, it looked like I was going to be living on airplanes for most of 1968.

"You Gotta Know the Territory!!!"

Borrowing a bit from "Rock Island," the opening song in Meredith Willson's "The Music Man," the local salesmen mock outsider Professor Harold Hill who "doesn't know the territory." In advertising as in all facets of marketing, you have to know the product, the people, the challenges and the opportunities. "You gotta know the territory!!!"

The M.O. of the agency dealer advertising proposals consisted of creating their quarterly local market ad programs with our copywriters, artists and media people in the Detroit office. I soon found out my dealers weren't very happy with this arrangement. Their co-op ad funds were paying for half the ad programs.

They, as well as I, wondered how the "creative" agency people in Detroit could understand the sales atmosphere or the car-buying climate in Kansas City or St. Louis. I'd always preached that what works in Los Angeles might not work in Nashville. The dealers had similar observations.

After "working the territory" and presenting a few Detroit-conceived ad programs to my dealers, I decided to take things in my own hands... customize the programs. *Job or no job. Boss or no boss.* I spoke with media people in the various markets to find out what was hot, TV, radio, popular and available within my budgets.

What was the local tie-in? Was there a hot new TV show with commercial availabilities, popular local sports event or radio DJ?

"If the Key Fits" campaign… a winner in the Twin Cities

I developed a successful car buyer prospect contest in the Twin Cities with huge newspaper ads and TV spots. The theme was for folks to go to their local Pontiac dealer and reach into a huge barrel filled with new car ignition keys. If the one you came up with fit the ignition on the Pontiac Grand Prix on the showroom floor, the payoff was a week at the very popular Playboy resort in Lake Geneva, Wisconsin. This was a period when Playboy not only published a magazine but they owned gambling casinos, nightclubs, a limo service and upscale vacation resorts. The "If the Key Fits" promotion brought tons of people to Pontiac showrooms.

The most effective local marketing promotion was the one I developed for Kansas City. I hooked up with Rick Roland, Marketing Director for the Kansas City Royals whom I met in the Kansas City airport bar. (What did I say earlier about advertising and alcohol? It goes hand in hand!) The Royals was a new American League team, started to replace Kansas City Athletics who had been moved to Oakland by the reviled owner Charlie Finley. There was no big time baseball in KC for two years until local pharmaceutical manufacturing tycoon Ewing Kauffman ponied up the money for an expansion team… the Kansas City Royals.

The Kansas City sports fans rallied behind Kauffman and demonstrated their enthusiasm for their new team by practically buying out the initial 1969 season tickets offerings. The Royals were now the hot item in KC. To capitalize on this fever I was able (with promotional promises) to get the ball club's head office to agree to make Pontiac the official car of the Kansas City Royals.

We, the Pontiac Division, gave the team eleven new models for the front office executives; LeMans, GTO, Grand Prix, Catalina, Tempest, Firebird. In return, my dealers received center field signage, mentions in Royals advertising and plenty of box seats for all the games to be used for customer promotions.

We had the use of the complete baseball team members for advertising. I produced a TV commercial at their spring training camp in Bradenton, Florida, where we showed the complete nine-man starting lineup pile out of a big Pontiac Bonneville station wagon to a recorded version of "Take Me Out to the Ball Game."

The fun part, for me was producing this spot with production facilities from a local Bradenton TV station and with no cost for talent the total budget for the commercial came in at $9,000… this at a time when Pontiac was spending $200,000 for 30-second network TV spot production.

A GM first… A Pontiac for the Kansas City Royals

The high point of my association with the Royals and our Pontiac dealer group was having the GM factory actually produce a special model just for the Kansas City market… for Royals enthusiasts. It was a royal blue Pontiac Tempest with special wheels, unique upholstery, some accessory frills and the Kansas City Royals nameplate on each front fender: KC ROYAL.

Pontiac Division executives told me that GM had never before produced a special, low-production-run model for a local market and we introduced it at the Greater Kansas City Auto Show. And the limited 1968 run was sold out quickly.

"Here Come the Judge!"

Also during this period Pontiac came out with a hot GTO, the Judge, which was a spin on the supremely popular Rowan and Martin's "Laugh-In" TV show tag line, "Here Comes the Judge." Timing was right for this hot rod as the tag line positioned the car as a muscle car… "Here comes the Judge" meaning "watch out dude!"

I knew it would be a hot seller with our seven dealers and I suggested they stock up. They did and were sold out in one weekend as the hot rod buyers took them out to the local drag strip. The 1969 GTO Judge cost about $7,000 and now can be found at major auto auctions commanding prices over $80,000.

The Royal's Omaha, Nebraska farm team was known as the Omaha Royals. I bonded with their GM Bob Quinn and tailored some promotions around his team. Quinn went on to become GM of the San Francisco Giants and Cincinnati Reds. Sorry I had lost track of him as we really hit it off… same age and lots in common.

Multi-tasking at its best

Via smoke and mirrors in 1969, I was servicing the seven Midwestern Pontiac markets while still producing my weekly live one-hour television show on Channel 26, Chicago, writing a weekly column for *Competition Press* magazine *(now Autoweek)* and racing my Healey, all while raising a family!

After two years at D'Arcy McManus ad agency in Chicago, slaving on the 140 Pontiac dealers' advertising accounts in Milwaukee, Minneapolis-St. Paul, Omaha, St. Louis, Oklahoma City, Kansas City and practically living on airplanes, I realized I wasn't getting any closer to my goal of working on the management and creative end of a major auto advertising program.

The tipping point came in late 1969, Ernie Jones, President of Darcy McManus told me he wanted to add the Denver Pontiac Dealers advertising association to my duties. Whoa! I'm a multi-tasker but even I know there are only 24 hours in a day. I didn't want to be a glorified errand boy for a bunch of car dealers. I wanted to make things happen.

Onward and upward to Detroit!

So, I mounted a job seeking blitzkrieg on Motown. I sent letters to the ad agencies for Ford, Mercury, Chrysler, Dodge, Chevrolet and Plymouth asking for an appointment. I drove to Detroit for a one-day series of sit-downs with the car agency personnel departments. Everyone was polite and interested but there were no openings.

Back to Chicago. At least I tried.

Two days later the general manager of Batten, Barton, Durstine Osborn (BBDO as they are known in the business), ad agency for the $40 million Dodge account called me. He said Dodge president Bob McCurry had instructed the agency to find an account supervisor for the auto company's high-performance car line.

Seeing that I was currently working on a major car account, produced a motorsports TV show and actually raced it seemed I'd be a candidate. Could I come to Detroit right away to interview? Here it was… my dream job.

In 1969, that meant the obvious move: Detroit. *UGH!* That city had a worse crime rate than Chicago. It was blighted, dirty and angry. Nobody strayed in downtown Detroit after dark and you were a robbery target merely walking to your parking lot car after work. But was the car capital of the U.S. It was where new models were created, built and marketed. I wanted to be a part of the big picture and make an impact.

Two days later I'm in the reception room of BBDO waiting to see John Wilson, head of the Detroit office and the $40 million Dodge advertising account. WOW … *the big boys!* I'm about to meet one of the movers and shakers of the automotive advertising fraternity. *Oh yeah!*

So this is Detroit?

What a joke… on me. I'm expecting a John Z. DeLorean, Edsel Ford clone… the original man in the grey flannel suit… smart, well groomed… a real cool car guy. I walked into the Wilson's corner office and there he's slumped, clad in a Hawaiian shirt, shoes off, feet up on his desk right next to a bottle of Pepsi (a BBDO account), a bottle of Early Times and he's listening to Hawaiian music. We sat down to chat.

Ah, the big time??

It went well. Wilson knew nothing about the high performance side of the car biz but Dodge Boss, Bob "Captain Crunch" McCurry had given orders to hire a performance car guy and here I was.

Wilson asked me to stay over in Detroit to meet McCurry the next day. Get a hotel, toothbrush… get it done. I did. I met Crunch and it was great. We bonded. I had attended two Big Ten universities and McCurry was nominated for All-American linebacker at Michigan State. To make things even better, he loved racing.

After that, I was asked to meet the head of Dodge PR, Frank Wylie, an extremely knowledgeable guy on motorsports but a pain in the ass to work with. He thought he had all the answers and was constantly attempting to one-up anyone to display his superior (?) knowledge. **I took the job!** It still it meant leaving Chicago, my hometown, and my TV show "Motorsports International."

*Screw the agency protocol… we need a campaign… **NOW!***

I came back a few weeks later to take over my new position, new office and meet the rest of the BBDO Dodge advertising team; the account supervisors, my assistant/photographer Bob Osborne, art directors and other dealer ad association account executives.

I got along just fine with the team but noted a bit of jealousy. A big part of my job was to attend all sorts of motorsports events in the US including Daytona stock cars in February; Riverside in California, drag races, car shows… any place Dodge cars were racing. Dodge paid for all the expenses. So while my agency associates were freezing in Motown in February I'd be in Florida or Alabama for a car race.

For the first major Performance Cars ad campaign, 1970, I faced a very tight media deadline for the program, which included Dodge Charger, Hemi Charger, Dart Swinger, Dodge Super Bee, and high winged 200 MPH Dodge Daytona and the new Dodge Challenger pony car.

In many big ad agencies (at least during this period) and especially at BBDO, account executives have no say so regarding the creative process. The creative director informs everyone that he runs the show. He *is* the agency and no martini-swilling, expense account AE's were giving him orders. It's up to him to make deadlines and create magazine, newspaper, radio and television advertising. My creative director was a guy named John Van Dagens. He ran his own little fiefdom of writers. Nobody was about to tell them how and when to do that job.

Plus the top consumer car magazines, *Road & Track* and *Car & Driver*, I was agonizingly aware that our new ad campaign for the high performance car line must kick off in all of the Peterson Automotive Publications - *Hot Rod, Motor Trend, Rod & Custom, Sports Truck* - within a few weeks. To add a big dose of pizzazz to our program, I had the media guys order eight page inserts in all magazines; a 48-page 4-color blockbuster for all the new hot cars and introduce the newly formed Dodge Scat Pack Club designed to offer Dodge high performance enthusiasts special deals on racing accessories and race gear.

Van Dagens and his wordsmiths kept ignoring my pleas for copy. "Yes, we're getting to it. Don't tell us what to do."

Finally I thought, "Screw it. I'll create the 1970 campaign myself. Let the chips fall where they may."

Head dude John Wilson was still sitting in his corner office swilling down Pepsi and Early Times. He didn't care what we were facing. I sat down at my trusty Royal typewriter and came up with the theme… an unconventional and creative approach. The client liked it and bought it.

At this particular time in auto advertising, the feds were clamping down on any mentions of speed, street racing or horsepower so we were handcuffed as to how much high performance info we could shout out in our advertising.

*My biggest thrill was going out to the Dodge plant in Hamtramck, Michigan getting out of my car and looking up to see a 40-foot banner across the top floor of Dodge Main announcing **"WELCOME TO SCAT CITY."***

I came up with the headline **"WELCOME TO SCAT CITY."** This is where Dodge performance cars were developed and tested. Scat was a spin on popular reggae singer Johnny Scat Davis and to any hot football halfback who was a "scat back." Scat City was a mythical place... and it was where hot cars were being made and tested.

I wrote the eight-pager which included the newly developed Dodge Scat Pack Club where you could get all your Dodge performance goodies.

Despite Van Dagens and his lemmings, the client bought the program, which we supplemented with more magazine ads, newspaper ads heralding Dodge racing victories plus radio commercials.

The Dodge Challenger Pony Car and Pikes Peak

One of the most rewarding campaigns was the "Climb to the Clouds." I talked client Dodge division Chrysler Corporation into hiring four time Indy 500 winner Al Unser, Sr. to attack and break the speed record for the oldest automotive competition event in the US... the July Pikes Peak Hill Climb, "The Climb to the Clouds."

We were debuting the Dodge Challenger and it seemed it would make good PR to challenge the Peak with the Challenger...
Mom, Apple Pie, the Flag and Pikes Peak.

As the Colorado-based Unser family owned just about every Pikes Peak speed record, Big Al (Al Jr. was "Little Al") was our logical choice. Unfortunately two weeks prior to the event he fell off his bicycle... Yes, his bicycle... in the pits at the Indianapolis 500, broke his leg was put out of commission. End of our Pikes Peak project.
I did attend the event to scout it for the following model year.

Also I followed the initial phases of "prepping" the Challenger race car for a season of competition against Ford Mustang, Chevy Camaro, AMC Matador, Pontiac Trans Am and Plymouth Barracuda. You start "prepping" the race car by taking it completely apart and "acid dipping" the entire metal body. This takes off weight. Then the 340 ci motor is destroked to 315 ci and rebuilt to add at least an additional 100 horsepower over its stock power curve.
Speed costs money!

"You in a heap of trouble, boy"

Remember those great Dodge Sheriff TV commercials of the 1970's? These were the ones where the Dodge "Safety" Sheriff would pull a motorist driving a new Dodge Charger or Challenger over to the curb and say, "You in a heap a trouble, boy… Seeing how's you're driving this racing car on city streets…" I was a member of the Dodge account management team that created the account.

The driver-actor explains to the Sheriff that this is the new Dodge Challenger sports car. The ad program got raves from the industry and created car sales.

Here's how this campaign evolved. The commercials were created, written and Dodge client approved. But we did not have the key ingredient… a redneck cop … that is until one day, in Hollywood, the agent for movie character actor Joe Higgins contacted the ex-Air Force Colonel Higgins as he was putting in his monthly U.S. Air Force Reserve flying hours at an airport near Los Angeles.

He was told to drop everything and head on down to the BBDO office on Wilshire Boulevard immediately for an interview.

Joe was in his Air Force uniform complete with 50-mision crush officer's cap. He looked like a rural cop.

When Joe walked in wearing his military uniform and said, "You in a heap of trouble, boy." The job was his.

*"Big Daddy" Don Garlits… No less than
"The Second Coming" for Some Detroit Kids*

The biggest name in drag racing has been and always will be "Big Daddy" Don Garlits. Billed as the "Swamp Rat" from Sefner, Florida, Garlits ruled the roost in the wildly popular high horsepower sport of drag racing. Quarter mile nitro methane powered Top Fuel Dragsters were sling shooting to speeds over 200 MPH in 1320 feet… the quarter mile.

Trick monikers for the daredevil drivers were attracting young race fans by the thousands to hundreds of sanctioned drag strips in every state.

"Dyno" Don Nicholson, Shirley "Cha Cha" Muldowney, Don "The Snake" Prudhomme, "Dandy" Dick Landy and Tom "The Mongoose" McEwen were racking in big bucks and Garlits was the king… the first racer to do the quarter mile in 170 mph, 200, 240, 250, 260, 270 mph… all this back in the 60's and 70's.

At 71 years of age he ran a 319 MPH quarter mile at the Gatornationals only to be beaten by my Newport Beach, California neighbors, Kenny Bernstein's son Brandon in his Top Fuel Dragster. Big Daddy Don remains a major attraction at National Hot Rod Association (NHRA) events nationally.

While preparing my 1970 Dodge high performance national ad campaign, I decided to bring in the top Dodge racers from all over the U.S. and photograph them at race venues near Detroit as they were wringing out the new models.

Garlits flew in from Florida and I met him at the Detroit airport. We headed for Michigan International Speedway in the Irish Hills 65 miles west of Detroit. The two-mile semi banked track was one of the newest and fastest race venues in the U.S. and Indy Cars had been lapping it at 220 mph… the perfect background for automotive high performance photography.

I was driving a non-descript four-door Dodge Monaco company car with no visible performance features. It was sort of a plain travelling salesman's four-door sedan.

We stopped for gas at a small Shell station in Hobart, Michigan about 40 miles from the Speedway. I noticed a hopped-up pickup truck sitting next to the gas station that appeared to be owned by the attendant or some of his buddies who were inside chewing the rag. I heard race jargon.

The truck had custom wheels, flashy paint, chrome exhaust tips... sort of a starter kit for junior hot rodders.

I knew it was Big Daddy time... thought I'd have some fun.
So I went in and said: "Neat truck... what'll it do in the quarter mile? Have any of you guys ever heard of Big Daddy?"

In a unified chorus they all said, "Heck, who hasn't!"

Show time.

"Big Daddy" Don Garlits, champion of the drags.

"See the guy in the passenger seat of the Dodge outside? That's Big Daddy."

You would have though I just told them the Pope was paying them a visit. They couldn't believe the one and only Big Daddy Don Garlits was in their presence.

They'd read about him setting fantastic speed records in Florida and California. Here he was… in the backwoods of Michigan… in person… in their gas station.

They stood around my car and stared in disbelief. Being the cool guy he is, Big Daddy rolled down the window and talked drag racing while I pumped gas. These kids were in heaven. He gave them all tickets to a race in Muskegon, Michigan coming up in a few weeks.

The regard these kids had for this iconic racing idol was unreal. And, of course, I really knew I'd selected the right racing personality to represent the new Hemi Dodge Charger.

It would have been interesting to hear how they explained their "audience" with Big Daddy Don Garlits to their buddies back in the high school cafeteria.

They were certainly celebs for a few weeks. I'll wager the four-minute confrontation took 40 minutes in the telling.

CHAPTER ELEVEN

Bye-Bye Scat City! Hello Windy City! Home again!

I thought the BBDO Detroit job supervising the high performance/ racing end of the Dodge Division/ Chrysler Corporation was a dream job, but it was nothing compared to my return to Clinton E. Frank Advertising after five years in New York City and Motown. I'd quit Clinton Frank in 1959 when I realized I couldn't work with BS artist Perry Brand and heavy-handed, sleazy way of treating clients.

After my NBC-TV and New York City, Canadian Club and Chrysler experiences I received a call from my pal Gene Shields, V.P. on the Bissell ad account at Clinton E. Frank Advertising.

"You better get over here and see Clint as he just bought the Midwestern states distributorship for MG and Austin Healey. He needs an advertising and sales promotion honcho for the new multi-million dollar acquisition," said Shields.

Yep... right down my alley since I was engulfed in Austin Healey racing and was well informed and well connected to British Motors Corporation (BMC) marketing in the U.S.

A one-hour meeting with Clint was all it took. He finally realized that I quit his company several years prior because of Perry Brand's dubious business practices and that I was right. Clint understood because he had canned the jerk a couple years prior.

And I realized I needed to come back home.

Clint said "You're re-hired."

We may have to make you a separate division in the agency because there may be an account conflict. We have that new funny little Japanese car account in our Los Angeles office.

It's called Toyota!!!

"Let's call you W.J. Maloney Automotive Advertising Division of Clinton E. Frank, Inc." Little did he know about Toyota.

He had his office manager look for an office for me; he wanted to keep it away from the executive floor at the two-story penthouse offices of Chicago's Merchandise Mart. His office manager tried to find an empty office on the media floor but the only one available was an old storeroom filled with office supplies, Christmas decorations, old furniture and junk. I took it and when it was cleared out it proved to be the primo office in the entire ad agency. Nobody knew it had three huge windows facing the Chicago Loop, a faux fireplace and wall-to-wall carpeting. The furnishings included a massive desk, two couches, a coffee table, even a separate office for my secretary. My workplace was bigger than Clint's plush office but nobody knew it even existed.

There was no booze cabinet. Unlike most of the executive offices seen in AMC's "Mad Men," *nobody I knew in Chicago advertising had a cocktail bar in their office.* However like "Mad Men," depiction of office romances and fooling around with the help… well… that *did* exist. My daughter is editing this tome, so I'll pass on that aspect of the ad biz.

Chicago's famous Merchandise Mart, the World's Largest Office Building. When zip codes came along in the sixties, it was assigned its own!

Back to Clint.

To top it off he said, "What color new Austin Healey 3000
do you want?"

Talk about dream job! I had a generous ad budget and complete
autonomy since nobody at the ad agency had a clue as to what our
division was doing. I did sense a bit of jealousy among the account
execs. *And I had a new Austin Healey 3000.* Red, of course.

On weekends, I raced my Healey. In fact, I trailer-towed my race
Healey 3000 with my new street Healey 3000. It was a neat package
and made a grand entrance at Midwestern U.S. sports car racing
venues. All this was going on while I was still writing a weekly
motorsports column for *Competition Press.*

*NOTE: Today this publication is national weekly Autoweek, and
published by 32-title publisher Crain Communications.*

"The British Are Coming"

I created a hard-hitting ad program: "The British Are Coming!"
I instituted a sales incentive program that included trips to England
for our 55 Midwestern Austin and MG dealers. I created Port of Entry
(P.O.E.) sales where the car buyer selected his or her car right as it
arrived from England. We had overseas deliveries for buyers desiring
a tour of England and set-up a sports car racing cash contingency
program for owner/racers of MG's and Austin Healey's… they could
race an MG or Austin Healey. Those who did well in competition
got cash awards from Great Lakes car distributors.

Times were changing… the Japanese cars were here to stay!

At this point, I realized the day of the British made automobile was
going into the dumps. My secretary, Jan Wosniak, coordinated four
company cars for company executive business use: two MG 1100
2-door sedans and two of the new Japanese Toyota Celica sedans.
After a few trials it seemed nobody wanted the MG's so the
handwriting was on the wall. Toyota had arrived. The British
cars couldn't match the Japanese imports quality-wise. They lost
market share and finally British Motors folded and shut down
after producing sports cars and family sedans for 35 years.

Donald Healey… I was his "star" U.S. racer

In the world of sports cars, especially British sports cars, there is no name bigger than that of Donald Healey, the creator of the Austin Healey line of sports cars. He was a Royal Air Force Fighter pilot in WWII. When he returned to civilian life, he became consumed by the sport of auto racing and worldwide rallying.

In 1953, he developed one of the most beautiful two-seat sports cars to ever appear at an auto show: The Earl's Court Exhibition Hall auto show in London. The British Motors Corporation (BMC) bought Healey's company as they immediately noticed the sales potential of this new design. While it was sleek and pleasing to the eye, an anemic four-cylinder Austin tractor motor powered it. However, nobody cared… the car would soon be the hit of the 1954 New York Auto Show.

A winner.

I had always been an Austin Healey nut. When I finally got out of sports cars racing and restoring, I had owned seven of Donald's creations from the early four-cylinder AH 1004, a couple six cylinder 100-6 models and two A.H. 3000's.

While working on the Austin Healey advertising account for Clinton E. Frank Agency, I took trips to England and the assembly plant at Abingdon-on-Thames. While there in 1968, I had the privilege of spending some time with Donald Healey. I found him to be a very interesting, warmhearted and gracious gentleman. *Motorheads always bond.*

Mr. Healey set me up with a visit to the BMC competition department which was just winding up a banner year in worldwide rallying with their aluminum bodied Austin Healey 3000's. It was the same model as the two-seater I was racing but had exclusive factory modifications for speed and handling.

I received a hearty greeting by David Frederiksen, Competition Director. He told me to pick out any racing pieces used by the factory teams that I might want to put on my AH 3000 race car. Why me?

Why was I getting such preferential treatment?

I was a kid in a candy store and could not believe my good fortune. After loading up boxes of special spark plugs, carburetor parts and shock absorbers, I zeroed in on a very expensive one-of-a-kind aluminum cylinder head called a Westlake head, the same cylinder head designer doing the modifications on Dan Gurney's Formula One Eagle race cars.

I was in heaven.

I was told to go to BMC's London office to receive customs and shipping documents. I kept wondering why these guys were being so nice to me. Why did I get all this good stuff? **Free!**

While waiting in the reception room for my shipping documents, I picked up a copy of the BMC's worldwide monthly publication, *Safety Fast*, and there I was on the cover! The shot was of me winning an important sports car race in St. Louis as I blasted under the MG Austin Healey overpass bridge. Apparently, in their eyes, I was a U.S. racing star; the "Mario Andretti of the "sports car set."

When I got back in Chicago, I was going bonkers waiting for my shipment to arrive from England… It finally got to O'Hare Field and I rushed to my race garage in Gary, Indiana to show my mechanic, Jim Collins, our new-found speed largesse… and we installed the hopped up parts on my Healey. We were ready to rock and roll to the most famous and fastest racetrack in the U.S… Daytona International Speedway.

Porsche Spoken Here… 1964

Of all the hundreds of magazine, newspaper ads, radio and TV commercials I've created my number one favorite is an obscure, tiny "reader" type newspaper ad for the U.S. Porsche Dealers Association. The ad was a mere two columns by three inches and said, *"PORSCHE SPOKEN HERE"* and gave the name and address of the dealer.

That says it all. Even today I think this concept could make a neat Super Bowl ad. No audio… just pictures of Porsche models, technicians, dealerships… an aura of Teutonic engineering and performance. This was one of my freelance ads.

CHAPTER TWELVE

California Here I Come!

You become a freelancer for a reason. Either you get pissed off at your current employer and quit *or* got fired and say, "Screw the job hunting scene because now is my chance to go it alone… to make all my great ideas come to fruition." In my case, it was the former: to leave the structured ad agency system and to develop my television concepts to see if they were doable and marketable.

To be a freelance or independent TV producer takes more than a basic knowledge of creating a video or TV program; throw in scripting and production activity including casting, script, wardrobe, funding, airing, union rules, etc.

Knowing the nuances of video production is only half the battle. If you're going to be an independent producer, you're going to have to be able to sell. You'd better have some marketing skills including knowledge of demographics, of target markets, prospective clients, audience projections and, of course, attractive cost structure for your project.

I felt like I had all the skills, I just needed the opportunity. So in 1970, I uprooted my family and headed west, to California, where I opened a storefront office in Newport Beach.

U-505 submarine story for network TV, "Away Boarders" 1973.

While brainstorming an automotive television show concept with Herman Saunders (former executive producer of the top rated Cop TV series "Adam 12" starring Kent McCord and Martin Milner) I mentioned that I had in my possession a 16 mm film (it was actually Admiral Daniel Gallery's personal Navy classified film) of the actual World War II capture of the German Submarine U-505 off the coast of French West Africa in 1944. I told Herman I thought it was a great war story; a patriotic Navy recruiting vehicle.

Herman had a bungalow at the Raleigh Studios in Hollywood just down the street from the famous Formosa restaurant and watering hole on Melrose Avenue, second only to the Brown Derby in show biz popularity.

This is where we lunched and chewed on new program ideas. However our car show conversation was shelved when I related the true story of the dramatic capture of the Nazi "untersee boot"… the treacherous U-505 German submarine.

Would this high seas escapade make a good TV epic? It seemed to have all the ingredients: heroic American gobs, defeated German sailors, real action on the high seas with an aircraft carrier, destroyers, fighter planes, depth charges and machine guns… even a torpedo shot.

We screened my personal copy of the 'formerly classified' Navy documentary of the high seas escapade. Saunders' head writer John Fredericks came up with a great concept for a two-hour TV special.

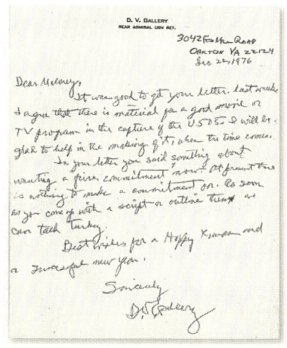

Handwritten letter from Admiral Gallery giving his blessing to the U-505 TV project.

With the U-505 capture as its centerpiece, Fredericks wound an exciting narrative around the event. He added characters, incidents, places and a moving story that not only culminated with the boarding of the booby trapped sub but had an unbelievable surprise ending. This is the same formula employed in making the movie "Pearl Harbor," "A Bridge Too Far," and even "The Alamo."

Fredericks came up with a five-page treatment with a working title "Away Boarders," a term the American Navy had not heard since the War of 1812. He created an Ernest Hemingway type war correspondent who, to his chagrin, was assigned to cover the unimportant Hunter-killer Navy Task Force Group 22.3 operating in the North Atlantic.

The once famous correspondent was despondent, hadn't had a scoop, a headline, or a big-time war-story in two years. His star was fading; he was being forgotten by his contemporaries at all the Harry's New York-type bars/watering holes around the world.

However all is not lost, he told himself. This may be a minor Naval mission, but it's headed by an ambitious, gung ho, full-speed-ahead Navy skipper with an eye for headlines, Captain Dan Gallery.

The pinnacle and high point of the proposed two-hour movie took place when Captain Gallery's task force successfully captured the German submarine and discover they've also captured the secret Nazi Enigma code as well as a brand new German acoustic torpedo. This was high drama as this stuff was super-secret. D-Day was just around the corner. The day was June 4, 1944, 150 miles off the Rio de Oro, French West Africa, two days before the Allied Invasion of Normandy... D-Day!

We depicted the action exactly as it happened in World War II. The only fictional element was the war correspondent.

In the final scene of the movie, we see our energized war correspondent diligently typing away, wrapping up his WWII scoop masterpiece and then heads for the flight deck of the U.S.S. Guadalcanal and Skipper Dan Gallery. Behind them the U-505 silently slides through the waves attached by cable to the aircraft carrier.

He excitedly tells the Captain that this is the big one. This is the scoop that will finally get him back to the literary big-time where he belongs. Pulitzer calls. It will immortalize Dan Gallery and his men. This, the U-505 capture, is one of the greatest stories of WWII.

He shows his 20 pages hastily written story to the Captain and says, "It's time to file. I have to go now and wire this to the Associated Press and my publisher."

Captain Gallery looks the veteran reporter in the eye and sadly takes the manuscript out of his hands and throws it into the ocean and says, "I've just received word from the War Department. This operation is Navy classified until the war is over… I'm sorry."

Roll credits.

Veteran actor Jackie Cooper gets involved… a true patriot

Back to Saunders.

Saunders knew former child actor and gung-ho Navy Reserve Captain Jackie Cooper, who then had a program development contract with ABC-TV. He was confident our proposed movie would appeal to the ex-child star turned director.

I also knew that Cooper, like me, was an Austin Healey nut. At that point I had owned five of the British sports cars and had done a lot of racing. I remembered that Jackie Cooper was no slouch race-wise and had participated in some very important high-speed Healey endurance tests with Donald Healey and world driving ace Sterling Moss at the Bonneville, Utah Salt Flats.

We bonded and had several meetings where we laid out a presentation for the networks. We were sure the Navy public affairs people would love this program as a great recruitment vehicle. I started making contact with the Navy to renting a sub, Baby Flattop, Destroyer Escorts.

Though the rental prices were insanely high, renting was doable. The nearest submarine was the one used in the Cary Grant movie, "Operation Petticoat." It was dry docked nearby in Long Beach.

We needed Admiral Dan Gallery's OK and we got it.

A plan to debut "Away Boarders" in Chicago

We got a promise of the Navy's cooperation as well as the Chicago Museum of Science and Industry where the sub now rests. At this point in 1973, about nine million visitors had already been through the U-505 exhibit in Chicago… a ready-made audience for our movie.

They've seen the submarine. Now they could watch it in action on the big screen. We buttoned up the representation and Jackie ran it by the folks in the "Black Tower" as the HQ building is called at ABC Hollywood.

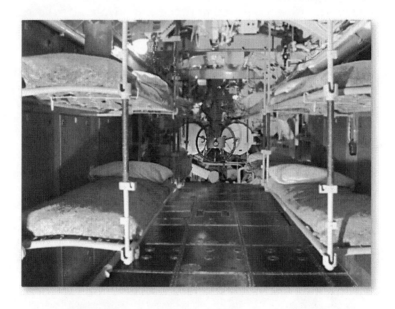

Sleeping quarters inside U-505. The 59 men slept in shifts.

Our timing was off. After a couple of weeks of to and fro, the ABC program execs said that there was a sudden flood of war epic presentations and they had just green lighted the "Raid on Entebbe," a two hour made-for-TV special with Peter Finch, Martin Balsam and Charles Bronson. They would have to pass on our high seas proposal.

Obviously Cooper and I were pissed off and wished our timing had been better but thought we'd forge ahead and take the treatment to another network as it was planned, budgeted as a made - for TV production not a feature film.

But Cooper got caught up in another project and we sort of lost interest. Shoulda… coulda.

And that was that for the "Away Boarders" story of the U-505.

The Olympics, 1984

I took on a project for the 1984 US Summer Olympics for a Hispanic-owned Costa Mesa, California company that made sports apparel.

I soon learned that it was extremely difficult to obtain an Olympic marketing license.

Fortune 500 companies seemed to own all the "official" categories: the official soft drink was Coke, the official candy bar was Hershey, the official breakfast cereal was Wheaties, etc.

However, there was a lesser-cost co-sponsor category we were going to aim for.

I hired 1968 Olympic Decathlon (Mexico) champion Bill Toomey to represent the client who was also sponsoring my KDOC-TV Anaheim Motorsports International weekly television show.

The highlight of my Olympic experience was traveling to the Olympic village in Colorado Springs carrying a cashier's check for $300,000, my client's down payment for their Olympic marketing license.

Toomey was a barrel of fun… a really good guy. He introduced me to ex-U.S. Senator and two-time U.S. Olympic Decathlon champ, Bob Matthias, (1948, London; 1952 Helsinki) who at that time headed up Olympic Village.

Working on the Olympic Games marketing was exciting and enlightening as the marketing side of the corporate program was almost overwhelming.

I attended meetings at the Olympic Training Center with CEO's, marketing directors of almost every Fortune 500 company including Coke, Dow, Kellogg's, Panasonic, G.E., McDonald's, Budweiser, Visa, United Airlines, Proctor & Gamble.

I added up what I knew about their marketing budgets and it totaled in the billions. Rarified atmosphere. Good games. Our client was happy and sold a ton of Olympic t-shirts.

CHAPTER THIRTEEN

What does an executive producer do?

I've been the executive producer for many, many TV shows over my career. Maybe this is a good place to explain what an executive producer does. Who is this Bill Maloney, executive producer?

Basically, the executive producer in the world of television is the person who finds the money for production. There's more to this title because often the producer most likely is the one who dreams up the concept for the property or teams up with someone who has the rights to a program… but needs money and connections.

"CARS N STARS," the Los Angeles Auto Show

Here's how I developed the "CARS N STARS" one hour television special for ESPN for Los Angeles Auto Show in 1990.This was the last of three network TV specials of the Los Angeles Auto Show I produced.

There are over 100 auto shows in various cities in the U.S., but four of these are the major shows: Los Angeles, Detroit, Chicago and New York. These are the big stages where automakers present next year's and future models.

The major shows compete with each other for manufacturers' unique exhibits and newest unveilings. The best presentations draw larger paying audiences and more auto journalists for pre-show press meetings and previews.

With this in mind, I was positive the Los Angeles Auto Show executive Andy Fuzzesi would welcome my planning and producing a network TV show around their auto show. No licensing fees were involved since the show would be promoting attendance at this great New Year's kick off show.

Next on my agenda was to interest a TV network in taking the program if it was network caliber production. I hired local independent TV director-editor John Kerwin, an ex-NBC production guy who had a fishing show running on ESPN.

I had worked with him on a TV pilot show when he was a part of Fawcett-Kerwin Productions in Orange County. Though that production was a debacle (Chapter 15), the blame rested on Fawcett. John knew the ESPN brass and they knew he could deliver a good show.

Now we needed a couple of marquee TV hosts... knowledgeable car guys with lots of network TV experience and an audience following... the type of national visibility a network would opt for and a title sponsor would buy into. The two hot guys at this time in the world of TV and cars were veteran car TV guys Bob Varsha and his sometime sidekick, former Formula One and Indy 500 racer David Hobbs, a couple of well-known personalities.

To theme the show (make it sponsor saleable and more than an infomercial for new cars), I knew that most automakers participating in big time auto racing had deals with their nationally known drivers that included PR and TV appearances. We needed a high performance look and feel. I was confident we could get super stars Richard Petty, the Unsers, Don Garlits, Parnelli Jones and many others to appear on the show I now named "CARS N STARS, 1991... The Los Angeles Auto Show."

Kerwin, because of his affiliation with ESPN, was able to get their programming department to offer us a good time slot based on my being able to obtain a sponsor for the show. There were to be two airings; the first show being late the same evening of our productionand a repeat four days later.

This would be nearly impossible as it meant shooting nine hours with automotive journalists, press preview day with a ten-man crew, two cameras, prompters, and miles of cable. Tough assignment.

I hired Kevin Smith from *Motor Trend* Magazine to handle the script which basically was dialogue for our "stars" and descriptions of the new cars... sports cars, SUV's, luxury cars, exotic cars, family sedans and most importantly the cars of the future; the concept cars.

Now I had to find an advertiser to bankroll the production and time cost. A title sponsor pays for the entire production and the network gives me, the producer, four 30-second spots to sell and I keep the revenue...my profit.

Yokohama Tire Company's U.S. headquarters was just down the road in Fullerton, California. I put together a presentation consisting of a look at $100 million new cars, racing stars, prestigious TV network, good time slot with a rerun... $200,000 and they bought title sponsorship of the program. Now we had to produce the show.

Kerwin arranged for the huge production semi-trailer where he and his TD and technicians worked on the script and prepared the teleprompter.

We rocked and rolled. What a project. It actually did take 14 straight hours of shooting and more time for editing. Somehow we got the finished product up on the satellite to Bristol, Connecticut in time for the network to air it nationally late Saturday night.

It was a pressure cooker. Then we partied. Yokohama was happy as well as the other sponsors, All State, Mars, Goodyear and Bank of America. As for me... never again.

"Let's Talk Law" – another first

About this time I had an idea for a series of home videos about what to do before you spend money for a lawyer. I went to my local library and asked them if they had any law books.

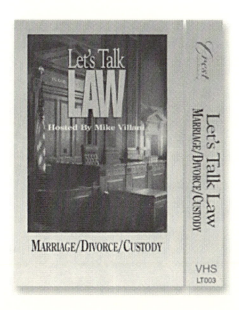

The librarian said "Of course. We have hundreds."

I asked if they had any video tapes about law. It turned out they had one… restaurant law.

I saw a niche and decided I'd try to occupy it with a series of basic law videos designed to help people save money before they saw a lawyer. The titles were: *"How to Select a Lawyer;" "Small Claims;" "Marriage, Divorce, Custody;" "Problems in the Workplace;" Bankruptcy;" Criminal Law."*

I thought I had a handle on marketing. I was under the impression that libraries, my initial targets, purchased products en masse. For example, I thought the 15 local libraries in Orange County, California purchased their books and materials as a group. I was wrong. They bought stuff one or two at a time, library by library.

That was a drag sales-effort wise. I had a video marketing company handling my law videos but they weren't about to call on 1,500 libraries.

However we sold some and got great reviews in *Variety* and we probably broke even production cost-wise. As far as I know this was another *first* as there were no videos in libraries covering law subjects.

We shot the six 40-minute tapes in two days with local hot shot TV commercial personality Mike Villani hosting. He pre-recorded the entire 200 plus minutes of dialogue using a unique ear prompter that allowed him to look into the camera and repeat what he heard from his earpiece.

He talked and talked and talked and after two days he needed a long siesta. I attempted to learn the ear prompter but couldn't get the hang of it.

A "Fantastic Finish" with Meguiar's Car Care Products

As I warmed up to my job as producer/columnist for the newly organized *"The Auto Channel (TACH)"* bankrolled by Pennzoil, I was asked to create a new television commercial for Meguiar's car care products.

Located in Irvine, Meguiar's was a leading maker and oldest manufacturer of car polishes, founded in 1903. CEO Barry Meguiar was a pal.

I came up with a unique TV concept I titled "Fantastic Finish," featuring several Meguiar's products. I was able to find actual film of great automobile races that culminated in an ultra-close *fantastic* finish.

One was the 1990 Al Unser Jr. victory over Canadian competitor Scott Goodyear in 0.043 seconds at the Indianapolis 500 mile race… *the closest finish in Indy 500 history.*

The commercial pitch, *"Another Fantastic Finish."* And you can have a *"fantastic finish"* with Meguiar's Ultra Detailer. *Sell, Sell, and Sell!* The TV spot was successful and Meguiar's ran it for several months.

The power of radio advertising… and lawyers!

In 1999, Barry Meguiar asked me to create a series of radio commercials for Meguiar's and that's when I rediscovered radio… the *power* of radio… the *reach* of radio… the *immediacy* of radio and the *fun* of producing radio material.

Radio production took less preparation than did TV production but it held a creative challenge.

Meguiar's in Irvine was just down the road from *Road & Track Magazine's* headquarters in Newport Beach. *R & T* was one of the oldest most respected automotive enthusiast's magazines in the U.S. with over three million monthly readers.

R & T and Meguiar's… two good names. So why not produce a weekly *Road & Track* radio show sponsored by Meguiar's and air it on a major radio network? CBS radio had 160 stations and welcomed the idea *especially* when they realized *R & T* would promote the radio show to its millions of readers worldwide.

So I wrote and produced a pilot program with my concept and pitched it to CEO Barry Meguiar and to executive editor at *R & T*, Tom Bryant. Both guys loved the idea as well as the attractive time slot offered to us by the CBS radio network.

I thought this would be a great way to wind down my 40 plus years in the advertising business… still keeping occupied and still playing with cars. I knew I could bang out scripts, produce great one-hour weekly shows for *R & T* and Meguiar's each week and get paid for it.

We had an all-hands meeting with 17 people in the *R & T* conference room in Newport Beach where we laid out the program plans to everyone.

Barry Meguiar announced that he would even build a radio broadcast studio in the *R & T* building in Newport Beach.

The editors and the main players in the radio show wouldn't even have to leave their building to record their pieces each week. The show would feature new car reviews race reports, technical tips, personality profiles, concept cars, and classics… everything you read about in *R & T.*

Everyone involved loved the concept. I was pleased and the project was rapidly coming to fruition. To illustrate how cool it was to work with the folks at Meguiar's feature this: I had an update meeting in Meguiar's conference room with several of their staff, including PR director Leslie Kennedy.

As we went over budgets I said, "Leslie, isn't it about time some money changed hands? This is my concept and I probably should have some earnest money… something up front."

Leslie quickly responded, "Of course… How much?"

I said "how about $8,000?"

Leslie didn't flinch. She turned to her assistant, told her to "go to the accounting department and get me a check for eight grand for Bill."

Things were looking good for the radio show on all fronts until I pulled the boo-boo, faux pas of the century when I said to Barry, "We probably should legalize this project and have a contract between all three parties (Meguiar's, Hachette Filipacchi (*R & T* owner in New York City) and me). We need some sort of letter of agreement between all concerned."

Barry said he agreed and would call his corporate attorney.

We told Tom Bryant at *R & T* he should do the same.

And this is when everything went downhill…

and crashed.

Lawyers blew our beautiful project!

Meguiar's lawyers wanted their client to own the show.

Hachette Filipacchi, publisher of 39 weekly and monthly publications, also wanted ownership.

The game playing between lawyers went on for three months.

Impasse.

Hachette was a French-owned entity. Everything moved slowly. Even snowstorms in the Big Apple halted negotiations.

I was fuming. I could do nothing. Each entity wanted ownership of the property.

Finally, Barry said, "Bill, It's over… my legal bill is approaching $40,000 and I have to call the plan off. Sorry."

Next time = NO LAWYERS!

CHAPTER FOURTEEN

Famous People Have Encountered In This Crazy Life: *The Celebs*

Living in southern California and working in the television production business, I encountered a number of the greats and the ingrates.

> *Art Linkletter… he took time out for me while he was purchasing Australia*

While working on my U-505 submarine movie project, "Away Boarders" with Jackie Cooper, our script writer John Fredericks (who had written for "Adam 12" starring Kent McCord) told me that a friend of his in Newport Beach, California owned an advertising agency and needed some help in an automotive related ad account.

When ABC-TV decided to pass on "Away Boarders," I decided to look into the deal in Orange County. If you're going to work in Southern California, Newport Beach ain't a bad place to be living and toiling.

It seems that the ad agency needed an account executive for a mobile home manufacturer's association advertising account.

I had a pretty good track record in advertising promotions and TV production, which this project required, they made me an offer that included a new Oldsmobile Cutlass. I took the job in 1974.

The Western Manufactured Housing Association (WMHA) consisted of 18 western states mobile home builders. For the first time in their history, they agreed to band together and advertise the benefits of mobile home lifestyle and construction.

They had been spending around $150,000 in advertising.

By the time I completed a grandiose television proposal, they agreed to spend close to $3 million. The plan was to dramatically show that mobile homes were not flimsy egg crates but were nice, roomy, affordable places to live.

The cornerstone of my plan called for a TV host/spokesperson with solid credibility and believability. I made a list and called the agents for E.G. Marshall, Hal Holbrook and a few others. I wanted a solid, articulate person who would appeal to the "mature" mobile home buyer.

After three Hollywood agents told me to take a hike, I called Art Linkletter, figuring I'd get another agent. I really wanted Art for the job. He still had audience appeal and good visibility. He was likable and believable. On the plus side, Art owned several mobile home parks in the western states. I knew this would appeal to the client manufacturers.

We talked at length and I outlined the deal. I had a fee in mind that I quickly pulled out of the air. He needed to do three TV commercials, six appearances at manufacturers/dealer meetings on the West Coast and appear in a few newspaper ads.

Art was his own agent.

Art said, *"I don't have an agent. I don't need an agent. Let's talk."*

I went to his office and we struck a deal.

I seldom think of Art Linkletter as a TV performer, actor, a show host ("People Are Funny") and author ("Kids Say the Darndest Things"), but consider him a successful, hardheaded businessman.

He owned thousands of acres of land and thousands of cattle in Australia. He was on the board of MGM and the MGM Grand in Las Vegas. Besides owning mobile home parks, Art had a string of self-storage operations in a dozen western cities. He was a business dynamo.

Linkletter was accessible, cordial, on time and prepared for our television commercial productions.

The campaign for WMHA was a success. Art did his client appearances and was paid handsomely.

When it was wrapped up, I decided to do a weekend in Las Vegas and asked Art to use his influence to get me a super room at the MGM Grand and front row seats for the big gala in the main showroom. And he did but much to my chagrin, I didn't get a special deal. I paid the list price. *No freebies from chintzy Art who passed away at 97 in 2010.*

I'm certain he lived to that age because he *"kept on truckin',"* working at things like pitching mobile homes when he was a $zillionaire. He just liked to keep busy.

A funny thing happened during the shoot

We were producing one of our 30-second spots in a huge mobile home factory in Fountain Valley, California and Art was spokesman for the commercial.

For the second time in my executive producer TV career, I selected the wrong director to shoot commercials. He was someone's friend of a friend. The guy knew film but he was a dunce when it came to video. He'd cover his inabilities by reshooting and reshooting scenes so he had several to choose from… hoping to get at least one he could use. This irked everyone. We had a morning coffee break and Art excused himself to use the head. What he didn't realize was that his wireless lavaliere microphone was still live.

As I sat with the director and crew over a cup of coffee, we all heard Art in the men's room on his phone saying to his office, "Yes I'm here with a crazy ass director who doesn't know crap. So I'll probably be home *late.*"

Jay Leno… a smart and funny guy

I first met Jay Leno while I was working on a *Motor Trend* television show. I was immediately impressed not only by his funniness but more so by his complete knowledge of automobiles.

I bumped into him several times at major car shows like Pebble Beach. I was always impressed. He could talk to a car owner of a Duesenberg… or a Peerless… or a Bugatti… or some such historic classic… in detail about desmodromic valves, independent rear suspension, inboard brakes and ignition timing.

It seems that each time I dumped my auto-racing hobby (because it was too expensive or time-consuming) I'd be back at it a year later. Nasty habit. I figured vintage racing was now my game: Austin Healey, Elva Courier, Triumph Spitfire and Jaguar.

This was 1994. I was going through my annual "got to get back into racing" period and was looking for one of my Austin Healey race cars. A vintage racer friend in Pasadena said he thought that Jay Leno now owned the car. I sent an email to Leno's secretary, Helga Pollock, and asked her if she knew anything about my LeMans Healey. The next day my phone rang in Honolulu.

I picked it up and the man said, "Hi, Bill. It's Jay Leno and I have your Healey."

We rapped about how we met. He almost ran over me with his Ford Expedition in the Petersen Automotive Museum parking garage. I was working on a TV show he was appearing on at that time.

We talked for a while and he said that one of his mechanics John Parra, was restoring the car for vintage racing. To illustrate my auto astuteness, I told Jay to remind Parra that the car has a very rare custom intake manifold for two-side draft Weber carburetors and he should keep them with the car. When I owned the car, it took me a year to find… in Scotland.

Jay's Big Dog Garage.

Jay then suggested I stop by his Big Dog Garage at the Burbank Airport whenever I was in town. I did this twice, taking pictures I used on my "Ohana Road" TV show in Honolulu. At that time, Jay had about 50 cars and 50 motorcycles and today he has twice that number. It's a costly hobby and I strongly suspect NBC picks up the tab.

A year later, I had a TV sponsor who said he would bankroll my "Ohana Road" crew and me to cover the Los Angeles Auto Show which would air on the Armed Forces TV Network worldwide. I contacted the Marine Corps in L.A. and told them we could have a neat tie-in with Jay Leno and worldwide TV exposure. They jumped at it. Their recruiting people created a great looking "appreciation" plaque for Jay and one for Mark LaNeve, the Executive VP of General Motors. The GM public relations people set up a special pre-auto show TV shoot area for Jay with a new Daytona 500 Corvette. Two young Marines were to present Jay with the award plaques.

We assembled back stage at the L.A. Convention Center to tape the presentation. As soon as my two cameras rolled, some suit from NBC stepped in, put his hand over the camera lens and said, "No TV."

I said, "Knock it off. This is for the Armed Forces. These two Marines were up all night preparing this presentation."

The clown from NBC said, "No way. No TV unless it's NBC." Blah, blah blah. The GM PR people were embarrassed as was their boss Mark LaNeve. We were able to get a couple of still shots but that was it.

Dick Clark's Barbershop… all business kind of guy

About two blocks down Sunset Blvd from the Petersen Publishing building was the Dick Clark Productions bungalow. A friend of mine and of "America's Oldest Teenager", "Mr. American Bandstand" told me he was always interested in new TV productions and added that Clark had a part interest in an auto race track in Virginia. *My kind of guy.*

I *always* had a pitch for a TV series about cars… a spin on my Chicago "Motorsports International" show. Ready to rock and roll, I made an appointment with Clark. It seemed we had a few mutual acquaintances in Hollywood.

I went to his Sunset Boulevard office at the appointed time. I entered his executive office and found that the "visitor's chair" was a full-blown barbershop chair. And that's where I did my pitch.

The guy was *all* business. There were 30 seconds of pleasantries. I mentioned his racetrack, as maybe thinking this would get us on common *car guy* ground but found out it was merely an investment. No car enthusiast here.

I started to page through my flip-over presentation containing blowup photos of famous car people and sponsors who appeared on "Motorsports International. "

About a third of the way through my presentation he said, "Ok, ok. Enough of the buildup. What's the deal?"

This kind of deflated me. Not a smile in a mile. I gave him the pitch and he agreed to give it some thought.

Pretty cold dude. I never had any more contact with Clark but I did hear that "aloofness" was his normal behavior. I was told of one story of a writer who pursued him for an audience for weeks only to have Clark's bodyguard's car door slammed in his face. As he tried to talk with the *man!*

Billy Martin isn't amused by my Chicago Cop costume.

Billy Martin… he swung… I ducked

Billy Martin, the former New York Yankees manager was a great guy, despite his nicknames: "Enfant Terrible," "Battlin' Billy, the Bad Boy of Baseball." But there was this one instance. Billy loved to hang around the trendy, posh Balboa Bay Club in Newport Beach, California.

He was pals with the club's owner, Bill Ray, and could be seen making the rounds of some of Newport Beach's nicest and dumpiest saloons. I hooked up with Bill and Billy one afternoon as they were squiring "Mr. Inside," Army football team All American Fullback Felix (Doc) Blanchard (his halfback Glen Davis was known as "Mr. Outside" in the backfield), around some of Newport Beach's more infamous watering holes. Martin was a barrel of fun.

Each year The Balboa Bay club held a "Guys and Dolls" costume party where all the members and guests dressed like flapper floozies or Damon Runyon gangsters. Most people, Martin included, showed up looking like hoods.

For this party in 1990, I decided to make the scene dressed as a Chicago cop and scared the crap out of Martin when I tried to arrest him. He took a swing… It was actually dangerous… *but fun.*

Gene Hackman… fellow Journalism schoolmate at U of I

Gene was yet another film actor who was taking a shot racing a hot car around a racetrack. We were at Riverside Raceway's three-mile twisting road course, a *serious* race track.

He was hopped up about racing and told me he had recently invested a ton of money in a brand new race car design that proved to be a piece of junk.

As he said, "Bill, there I was arriving at the race track to see my new expensive race car get its shakedown run and it passes me going OUT of the track on a trailer and it's in pieces."

I had done my homework on his films and background and chatted about his recent roles and those on the drawing board. I asked him what movie of his he liked best.

He said, "I don't think I've done my best work yet." I told him I thought Popeye Doyle in "The French Connection" was fantastic.

Later, I found out Hackman and I were in Journalism school at the University of Illinois at the same time as was Playboy's Hugh Hefner who drew cartoons for the Daily Illini. I was writing some sports.

Laugh-In producer
George Schlatter

George Schlatter… a practical guy

"Laugh-In" producer George Schlatter was an interesting man, and though I only had two meetings with him, the circumstances and results were a learning experience for me in the world of Hollywood.

In the 1960's, George had been milling around the outskirts of show biz for some time and was manager of popular Sunset Strip nightclub, Ciros when the headliners were Martin and Rowan.

It was 1973 and I had developed a one-hour TV special for Robert E. Peterson of Motor Trend TV Productions called "The Golden Wheel Awards," hosted by James Garner. Originating at Caesar's Palace in Las Vegas, it was designed to be a network variety show with lots of Hollywood stars. The subject was automobiles with a series of awards for best cars in a variety of categories.

Once I had the production costs set, we felt we needed somebody with major network television contacts and experience to front this proposal to the big nets. I had meetings with Schlatter and told him I thought we could do the program for $200,000 and make money. He said that we should put a price tag $400,000.

I said, "Fine but why?"

George said, "It's a nice number." Just like that!

What I didn't realize before I met George was that he knew what the networks were willing to pay. I certainly learned something in my brief association with him.

The networks turned us down saying the program sounded too much like an infomercial for new cars.

Ruth Buzzi... holds her ground

Speaking of "Laugh-In... "Besides her weirdo roles, Gladys the crazy lady is basically a serious actress and accomplished comedienne. I was working on a new woman's cosmetic ad account that had some sort of orange ingredients that created a semi-facelift.

I wanted her to be spokesperson for our TV commercial. The idea was to show her as double ugly Gladys; then she becomes a beautiful woman after using this product. And she really was attractive.

I met with Ruth and her agent at a popular dinner club in Marina Del Rey near Beverly Hills and spent hours trying to convince her to do this commercial. She said Gladys was dead and buried and she never wanted to go back to that character again. She was pleasant, interesting, and funny but nothing would convince her to do our commercial. Good for Ruth.

Francis Gary Powers... a genuine personality

I had a couple of meetings with pilot Gary Powers a year after his return from Russia where he was shot down, imprisoned and accused of being a spy. I was attempting to talk him into making a TV commercial for a client wherein he would become the "eye in the sky" and a spokesman for the product.

He would be a homebuilder looking down from above saying, "Wow, look at all the people heading to Landmark Homes."

I believed every word Gary said about his U-2 plane and the weird circumstances that put him behind bars in Russia. He was a very warm and honest guy… a victim of the CIA's indifference.

Marsha Mason… in the "zone"

Ever since "The Goodbye Girl" and a couple other movies she made, I was in love with Marsha Mason. That is until I attempted to interview her at the Toyota Pro Celebrity Race practice session in 1997 in Long Beach.

While Robert Hayes, Merlin Olsen of the L.A. Rams, funny guy songwriter Paul Williams and other celebs including former two-time world driving champion Jack Brabham were completely cooperative in giving me TV interviews.

Marsha, who seriously wanted to become a race driver, sat in her car doing her Stanislavsky bit; psyching herself into a race mode (or mood) and she wouldn't talk to us.

She was communing with someone. She would not even acknowledge my TV camera/microphone and me as she was in orbit!

Screw Marsha.

Robert Hayes… hell of a driver

Robert Hayes, star of "Airplane," "Take This Job and Shove It" and a bunch of other neat movies was a delight. The reason his name sticks with me is that we chatted a great length of time at a celebrity race in Long Beach in 1997. His countenance, his delivery his look is that of a preppy weakling.

However when he raced, he blew away the whole field even challenging well-known Indy drivers for position. He was a charger. Like Superman, when he dons his cape, Hates turned into Mario Andretti when he put on his crash hat.

Songwriter Paul Williams served aboard U.S.S McCormick

My encounter with diminutive curmudgeon songwriter Paul Williams was brief but memorable. We were shooting videotape of a bunch of cars getting ready to go out on the racetrack for a celebrity event practice session at Riverside, California Raceway in 1997.

We came across a car that seemingly had no driver. Williams who is 5' 3" could barely see over the steering wheel. I mentioned to Paul that we had a mutual friend... the 6'7" comic, Pat McCormick. Paul said "Sure I know him. I served aboard him during the war."

Funny, funny guy.

Paul Newman, who didn't just play a race car driver on the big screen.

Paul Newman... wish we could have raced

I first met Paul Newman casually in 1968 at Road America racetrack in Elkhart Lake, Wisconsin. He was making the auto racing movie "Winning" (1969) where he played Frank Capua, a hotshot race driver.

It was here that Newman really got the racing bug even though he was in his forties.

I was at the track to observe and became one of the extras in a victory celebration scene at the finish line when Newman won a major Can Am race in a 600 hp Lola T-160 sports car.

We shook hands, chatted and that was that.

I really have to respect the guy for his driving ability. At forty years, he tackled sports car racing ferociously and he became a national champion.

I was getting serious about racing and Paul started competing in the D-Production class SCCA (Sports Car Club of America) "under three liter motor displacement" same as the category for my Austin Healey 3000.

I had a strong desire to race against him. *Strong.* I guess I wanted to be able to say, "I beat a movie star." But his racetracks were in New England and mine were in the Midwest. We never hooked up.

I bumped into him at a couple more racetracks including Riverside International Raceway where his professional racing team Newman – Haas was competing. His racing partner was Carl Haas, a Chicago friend of mine. I attended Carl's wedding.

At Riverside, I had a cameraman with me and asked Paul for an interview. He said he had to decline because if he gave one he'd have to give 25 more and he was here in California only to oversee his racing team.

And then I remembered why he formally opted out of the autograph business. A few years prior some clown followed him into the men's room of a New York nightclub and asked for his autograph as he straddled the urinal.

Newman decided then and there... no more autographs.

Bill Maloney talks with George Lucas at the Long Beach Grand Prix.

George Lucas… don't pass George!

Every year for 15 years, I attended the Long Beach Grand Prix Celebrity Race to do brief interviews with a great many interesting people. George Lucas liked cars but he was no racer.

He was a bit aloof but he had a great sense of humor.

Most of the participants in the annual Toyota Pro/Celebrity Race, (a companion race to the Toyota Grand Prix of Long Beach Indy Car race) the "celebs" are sports stars and quasi-TV celebrity soap opera actors who would give their first born to get onto the big screen.

They wanted to be recognized by Lucas.

He knew this and he also knew he was slow… slower than even the female thespians.

So he put a sign in the rear window of his little Toyota race car that said, "If you pass me, I won't hire you."

In-effective, but worth a few chuckles.

William Shatner... smashing up the expensive toys

Shatner tried his hand at the Toyota Pro/Celebrity Race at the Long Beach Grand Prix a couple of times with dismal results but he was a fun interview. His memorable line to me in 2006 was, "This is great fun. I can smash up a car and I don't have to pay for it."

A sprinkling of other celebs

Other celebs I found interesting who I taped and interviewed at the Toyota Long Beach California Grand Prix celebrity race each April starting in 1975 were Frankie Muniz, Charles Barkley, Indy 500 winner Rufus Parnelli Jones, Patrick Dempsey, Martina Navratilova, Merlin Olsen and Formula One world champion, Jack Brabham.

On the subject of celebrities... special individuals, my father would always say, "They're just like you and me.

They put their pants on one leg at a time."

But what he failed to point out is that all of these talented people worked very hard from their early years and for many years in their pursuit of a dream.

I respected all of them for being goal-oriented... and winning.

CHAPTER FIFTEEN

And there were the scoundrels

Rewind a few years to my first California office in a quaint business center replete with sculpted greenery and a babbling brook. One of the period cottages near my shop housed a company named Fawcett Kerwin productions, a company doing basically the same thing I was; TV and video production. Occasionally I'd stop in to see Bill Fawcett and John Kerwin and talk shop.

They had a neat operation with a campy screening room consisting of a dozen old flip up theater seats and wall-mounted video screen, rear projection, conference room, up-to-date AVID video edit bay, camera equipment room, secretary area and comfortable waiting room. They had all the stuff I did not have.

The well-rehearsed duo... all show and no go

The two guys, Fawcett and Kerwin, were a team; a well-rehearsed duo of hucksters with the dubious persona of a big time, high-powered TV production team.

Both handsome, well-groomed hot shots appeared as if they just stepped out of a Ralph Lauren *Gentlemen's Quarterly* page.

Both drove the latest top-of-the-line Mercedes Benz S Models. Yes, The Dynamic Duo. Unfortunately I was to find it was... as we say in racing... all show and no go. Though I initially took a liking to Kerwin, as we were both NBC alums, Fawcett was the head tap dancer.

Fawcett's executive office was huge and papered with celebrity pictures. He claimed to have at one time been CEO of Jack Daniels and even had a Jack Daniels commemorative bottle on his desk.

Later I found out this was BS. But at the outset I was really impressed. One day they introduced me to Dick Van Dyke who was taping an infomercial for a local home developer and many other big names.

Kerwin was an ex-NBC Unit Manager now working and living in Orange County. He did have a fishing show running on ESPN and seemed to be constantly on the go.

"Car Clinic" and the failed 7-11 deal

One day over lunch at Las Brisas in Laguna, I mentioned to them my "Car Clinic" property that I felt had a lot of promise. I told them I recently discussed it with the regional marketing manager of Chief Auto Parts, a 260-store division of Southland Corporation, which also owned the wildly profitable 7-11 chain of 4,000 stores worldwide.

I told the two TV guys that Chiefs' zone sales executive was really hot for the idea and wanted to take it to Southland management in Dallas as a network television possibility, paid for via co-op ad funds from Chief Auto Part's vendor's suppliers.

This could be a $40,000 per week deal for the producers.

Fawcett and Kerwin smelled big money and suggested we team up. Southland was the big leagues. They could do scripting, casting, work together on shooting episodes, editing, distribution and station relations.

It sounded pretty good to me as the next step would be to impress the huge Southland Corp that we were capable of pulling off a weekly "Car Clinic" TV show for them and their supplier vendors.

The ultimate smooth talker… and was he good!

When it came to presenting before a group, Fawcett had no peer. The guy was an actor's actor. He could give lessons to Dale Carnegie. This was his strong suit: pitching, selling, entertaining, promising, and impressing prospective client's customers. I soon learned, too late, that's where it ended. There was no substance… no follow through. He really thought he could actually snow his way into a sale.

I was still smitten with their operation and was readily willing to go along with any plan these two hustlers came up with.

"Yes, Bill," Fawcett said. "Let's call the VP of marketing at Chief Auto parts in Dallas as per his zone manager and get him to allow us to make a pitch for "Car Clinic.'"

I did the call and the Dallas exec said he loved our/my concept. He said he was going to be in Orange County the following week and wanted to meet with us. Hot damn… we are on our way. Fawcett Kerwin put their vaudeville sales act in motion.

"Get acquainted" sessions… California style

We scheduled dinner with the Dallas guy at Orange County's most exclusive and expensive restaurant, Chez Cary in Santa Ana. Reservations were tough to get. When you arrived, matchbooks (a smoking era) with your name engraved appeared at your table, as did footstools for ladies and a wine steward at your service. When you left the restaurant, your car was waiting at the exit, door open, and motor running. Very impressive and our prospective client from Southland was hooked.

Next he told us his boss would be in town soon and could we pitch "Car Clinic" to him. Of course. This involved more super entertaining as Fawcett Kerwin and me (and we split the bill three ways) rented an 80-foot pleasure yacht for a four-man Newport Harbor dinner cruise for the exec from Dallas. He was impressed and I really didn't know why since we still didn't have a script.

These were "get acquainted" sessions.

Southland then decided they wanted to get serious about "Car Clinic" and scheduled a big meeting in Dallas. They sent their company jet to pick us up at John Wayne Airport to take us to and from Texas.

We were hot to get the job done and prepared a 60-minute presentation on the look and feel of "Car Clinic" and where we felt it should be aired nationally.

When we got to Southland Corporation's conference room, we found marketing managers for all of their most important vendors waiting to meet us; Robert Bosch Spark Plugs, Monroe Shock Absorbers, Meguiar's Car Wax, Firestone Tires, Exide Batteries, Hurst speed equipment, Duco Auto Paints, Motorcraft Ford accessories, DuPont auto chemicals and others.

Fawcett, as I said, was a windbag… all show… but it was here in this situation that he absolutely excelled. He was introduced to seventeen executives he had never met before. First time. When, ten minutes later he faced the entire audience to kick off our presentation, he addressed each and every one of them by their first name. Unreal. They were stunned and obviously impressed. I sure as hell was.

"Bob, when we talk spark plugs the name Bosch… etc ."

"George, your company Monroe is the leader in shock absorber technology… etc."

"Ray, everyone considers DuPont as the industry innovator in… etc."

"Clyde, in tire technology Firestone has… etc."

To this day I don't know what trick he used to pull this off. How did he know all those names? Sure wished I could do that.

We left the meeting with $10,000 to make a 15-minute pilot of our show and had a due date for its completion. Hot dang. We are practically on the air. We went back to Orange County on the Southland jet with a feeling of invincibility.

The fun begins with production

Somewhere along the way I lost editorial control from these clowns. Now the fun begins as we have to produce and surely these two big time TV executives could produce a super pilot with my help. Though I was feeling more and more like the water boy following their suggestions.

Though Kerwin was an experienced video production director and editor he, like me, tended to follow Fawcett's recommendations for the production of the pilot. We interviewed actors, actresses and went from idea A to idea B to idea C and the whole thing became completely muddled.

Then with a client presentation date but three days away Fawcett (I went along like a dummy) hired a popular local radio DJ and sometime TV presenter to be host of "Car Clinic."

We found an old car and opened the show with this guy, Bill Huffman, popping out of the engine bay when the hood was open as he "greeted and announced" the format of the show. Then a series of actors peppered him with questions about auto repairs.

Pretty dumb.

I should have bailed but I was so enamored with Fawcett's super salesman powers I guess I thought he could actually sell this turkey.

No nonsense-marketing director sees through the BS

In the meantime, Chief Auto Parts replaced the marketing director we had been dealing with and who had been enjoying our profuse entertaining, and brought in a real no-nonsense auto parts sales veteran. He scheduled a trip to Newport Beach to screen and hopefully sign on for a 13-week series of "Car Clinic."

Showtime Fawcett style

Much to my amazement he hired a beautiful scantily clad gal model stringed harp player to meet the Chief ad exec at the entrance to Fawcett Kerwin Productions… strumming sweet music. It's 8:00 a.m.

A catered layout of champagne, coffee and pastries was offered and after introductions we settled in to screen the 10-minute video.

Usually in this sort of situation the client will come up with questions and announce that he will take a tape back to the home office in Dallas get back to us with a green light in about a week.

Not this new Chief Auto Parts executive. He saw it for what it was and said point blank, "This is a piece of garbage... we should get our money back... I came all the way from Dallas for this crap? Good bye."

And he left the office. That was the end of my possible association with Southland Corporation and a Fawcett eye opener for me. I thought I had learned a lot in Chicago, New York, and Detroit but I wasn't ready for the West Coast con artists. I guess I still had more to learn about hucksters and Hollywood.

Another scoundrel and Hollywood fraud!

One day my old BBDO/Dodge Detroit days pal, *Car & Driver Magazine* marketing exec Bob Brown, now publisher of *Motor Trend Magazine* called me saying that the TV division of Petersen Publishing (Robert E. Petersen Productions) needed some help with a national awards TV special they were developing. They needed a car guy with television production experience.

For a gearhead, working at Petersen publishing company could be heaven... new cars, racing, car celebs, travel, and excitement. I was hired to work closely with a guy named Jim Belcher, head of the Robert E. Peterson Productions TV division of Peterson Publishing, a company that published 15 monthly enthusiast publications including *Hot Rod, Motor Trend, Car Craft, Teen, Photography* and others.

Consummate car guy Bob "Pete" Peterson rose from the ranks as a photographer at the L.A. Times to create a billion-dollar publishing empire. Pete wanted to get involved with Hollywood TV show business and he hired Jim Belcher to run his video/film production company. The Peterson magazines operated out of a fashionable 15-floor office building on Sunset Boulevard with the TV production company situated in a two-story bungalow next door.

Belcher, a tall, well-coiffed, amusing and engaging character with a background as a stand-up comic, operated out of a plush office with several windows, couches and coffee tables, all befitting a Sunset Boulevard movie executive.

Next to his executive sized desk was a large flip-over easel stand containing a list of 15 TV productions currently "in production." Very impressive… and very Hollywood.

This guy has a dream job at a dream company. I was stoked… television and automobiles.

Love it.

Can this be for real?

Turns out it wasn't for real. Nor was Belcher. It didn't take me long to figure out that there were no productions in development and that the list of bogus program titles on his easel were there to impress visitors and other Peterson employees. There was no activity at Robert E. Petersen Productions though Belcher kept issuing "updates" on various projects.

Didn't know a car from a roller skate

Becoming more and more popular with Motor Trend's two million readers and Fortune 500 advertisers was the Motor Trend Car of the Year Award promotion. Pete thought this program was worthy enough to become a network television special awards show.

It would be exciting and profitable. He asked Belcher, head of his TV division to develop this program. Belcher, it turned out, didn't know a car from a roller skate.

And, as I found out later, had no clue about TV production. He was merely a pleasant-looking, funny, extremely vacuous dude. Fortunately for him I came into the picture.

I was hired as a consultant to create a TV awards special show… and I almost did. I saved his butt from the firing squad for several months.

The "Golden Wheel Awards"

I created an awards television show designed to air on a major TV network. It would be hosted by veteran actor and car guy James Garner (who I had interviewed for my Chicago TV show a few years before) and would originate at Caesar's Palace main ballroom in Las Vegas.

It would be a star-studded show. Because of Peterson's influence with all the major car company advertisers who spent millions in his publications, we figured funding for the production would be a slam-dunk.

We called it the "Golden Wheel Awards." We had trophies designed, budgets worked up, categories layed out and timetable outlined and went to Caesars to obtain their costs and cooperation.

Belcher, who I now am beginning to realize, is pretty much of a fraud, contributed zero to the development of this program.

In fact, he would spend his time taking trips to New York ostensibly to call on major ad agencies.

However, we found out later it was to take in Broadway shows, wine and dine his new wife and to shop for a new wardrobe… all on his company expense account.

He'd phone from the Big Apple to tell me about his meetings with Ford, J. Walter Thompson, and Young & Rubicam pitching new business. Later, we found out this was BS. There were no meetings. It was truly comical as he'd relate his conversations with agency executives. "I said… They said…" *In reality there were no meetings.*

Back to the "Golden Wheels Awards"… In order to interest the networks in this TV special we needed a front man…an executive producer with TV network connections. "Laugh-In" producer George Schlatter was available and I met with him.

Belcher said he was ill that day but in reality he didn't want to display his ignorance of TV production in front of George who was able to arrange meetings with the net's programming honchos.

As it turned out, the TV networks determined the program looked too much like a one-hour car commercial and turned it down so we put *"Golden Wheels"* on the back burner.

A pleasant sidebar in all this… Milt Payson

There was a humorous episode involved with creating that program. While working on the format I hired comedy writer Milt Payson. He was a trip. I remember he was working on a series of "bumpers" for our awards show; the brief segues between program segments that lead into a commercial. "Stay tuned… we'll be right back right after this from Ford."

Milt came up with a series of four visual bumpers that were a hoot. Bumper number one: an animated caveman carving a huge square rock. Bumper number two: the caveman had the edges of the rock rounded off. Bumper number three: caveman had of all it rounded and was working on putting a hole in the middle of the rock.

Now a huge round object with a hole in the middle (obviously the first wheel) and the caveman proclaimed joyously, "Look what I have invented. We'll call it… *FIRE!* "

Two successful programs produced without the scoundrel

I did manage to produce two programs at Peterson without Belcher! One was for British Leyland MG titled, "School for Speed" that was filmed at Riverside International Raceway. The other, "The Dream Team," a story of Parnelli Jones' Indy Race Team effort with Al Unser and Mario Andretti ran on ABC-TV.

Peterson bankrolled these shows and another production company produced them without Belcher. I made sure I was physically on the scene for both shoots. Belcher was a no show. Obviously he had no idea what was going on.

Belcher, realizing that his days at Peterson were numbered as in two years he had produced no programming or revenue, started job hunting.

All-Star Drag Racing Show...
and another scoundrel screw-up

While still a consultant at Robert E. Peterson Productions I came up with a concept for a weekly TV series called "All-Star Drag Racing" and it would involve the editors of *Hot Rod Magazine*. NHRA National Hot Rod Association and all the major high profile drag racers such as "Big Daddy" Don Garlits and Shirley "Cha Cha" Muldowney were ecstatic about this concept and we had several meetings... sans Belcher of course.

We had a meeting with 80 of the top drag racers in the country at the U.S. nationals in Indianapolis Labor Day weekend in 1973 to layout the program, and the drag racers embraced the project.

Peterson okayed a $25,000 budget for a TV pilot and he then took off for an African safari. He was an avid hunter. He had previously downed a10-foot grizzly with a pistol and the stuffed bear was the first thing to greet you when the elevator doors opened on the 15th floor of the Petersen Building. *Surprise!*

Pete left for the safari and we were planning for production of the pilot. Fred Waingrow, president of Peterson Publications, nixed the whole idea saying it was a Belcher pipe dream and the clown wouldn't be able pull it off.

I was still merely a consultant, not a full time employee and Belcher went to great lengths to keep me from interfacing with Pete or Waingrow.

Too bad.

It could have been a cool show as drag racing was wildly popular. So the clown affected my creativity and success as well.

Chilton comes calling… and he blows it again

Pennsylvania based specialty magazine and instructional manual company Chilton Publishing approached Belcher, so he said, to do a pilot for a new show about car repairs. I came up with the title, "Car Clinic."

Belcher convinced me that he and I should do this together, leave Peterson and make a bunch of money. As Peterson had Belcher's number and I was unfortunately seen as part of his team, I joined him in the Chilton project. Chilton is a big publishing company publishing 35 auto service manuals.

So I worked on it diligently for several weeks. When it came to pilot production time Belcher told me it was not approved so I left to work on my U-505 project.

Then I learned it was approved. He made a pilot and it was a disaster.

Chilton burned the videotape.

A lesson learned:

Belcher was the most blatant phony I've ever met in 50 years in the ad game. He conned Peterson out of a $100,000 down-payment to buy a new house adjacent to the Hollywood Bowl.

When Waingrow finally realized what a fraud he was and fired Belcher, the loan was forgiven.

The Petersen Empire *was a money machine.*

This was my worst "trusting" experience ever… a really bad no talent dude.

CHAPTER SIXTEEN

I've bench raced* a few professional drivers

*Commonly used term for sitting around and rapping about auto racing...
probably over a work bench*

Though the general public may not recognize many of the "all-stars"
in the world of motor sports, some who earn upwards of $30 million
per year, have personal managers and publicists. These men and
women are icons to their fans... the 40 million folks who purchase
tickets to auto races annually. The author has had occasion to rub
shoulders, break bread, hoist a Bud and bench race* with many
of the winners in what is sometime called "blood sport."

Carroll Shelby and the red bandana

Carroll Shelby was a motorsports icon responsible for the evolution
of the Ford Cobras and Lemans winning Ford GT 40 road-racing
rockets. At the behest of Ford CEO Lee Iacocca, Shelby created a
line of high performance sports cars to go up against GM's popular
and very fast Z-28 Camaro. I had the pleasure of introducing his
first Shelby Mustang on my Chicago TV show in 1965.

Carroll Shelby and his Shelby Ford Mustang GT

We filmed the interview, and I found him to be a real down-home Texas hot-rodder. I had dinner with him in New York City a year later and ran into him at various car shows and races every so often.

For some unknown reason, I started carrying a red cowboy bandana as my daily handkerchief. When people asked about this I'd reply, "It's great for cleaning windshields, checking oil… guy stuff… a signature thing."

My girlfriend, BG, thought it was just gross to carry a bandanna in a Brooks Brothers suit. While at a Meguiar's Car Care Products Company Christmas dinner in the 1990's at the posh Balboa Bay Club in Newport Beach with Karen and Barry Meguiar we were seated next to Cloe and Carroll Shelby.

Thinking I'd do a number on BG. I turned to Carroll and said "Yo, Shell… do you have a handkerchief?"

And he replied, "Hell, yes, Billy… here ya go." As I knew he would, he pulled out a huge red bandana and flashed it around… cowboy style.

So I turned to BG and, "SEE ? Big shots carry bandanas."

Shelby died in May 2012. We remained good friends throughout the years.

> *Rick Mears… one of the nicest guys in the auto racing business*

Only a few men have won the prestigious Indianapolis 500 four times. Bakersfield, California hot shot Rick Mears is one of them.

I first saw Rick in the race at Riverside Raceway many years ago where he crashed big-time. I thought to myself, "the guy should take up another hobby." *Little did I know?*

In 1978, I had a concept for a home video TV series on how to do your own car repairs. I knew I could get an auto parts company sponsorship. I was going to call it" Car Clinic" which is a cute title until you think, *"Who the heck wants to be involved with a clinic?"*

So I renamed the concept "TUNE-UP AMERICA." I needed a spokesman; one with credibility... that is, automotive credibility. I could see the face on the tape cover. My budget was really limited and though I yearned for Richard Petty, A.J. Foyt or Mario Andretti I knew I couldn't afford them.

Rick just had a bad racing accident in Canada and banged up both legs. His sponsorship had not been renewed for 1977, and I heard he might be going through a divorce. I figured he just might need some extra dough-re-mi.

I drove to Bakersfield to meet with him. I explained that I only needed him for a couple days work in front of the camera to introduce each of the "how-to" tapes on subjects like brakes, tune-ups, oil changes, bodywork, detailing etc.

We struck a deal and that allowed me to go to Pennzoil, Bondo, Monroe shock absorbers, Champion Spark Plug, and get them to pay for the production and the artwork required to make these tapes highly visible on the shelf.

We wrote the scripts, produced shows at a studio in San Diego with Rick and they turned out great. We actually sold a few. Mears was one of the nicest guys in racing I've ever met and is presently a consultant for Roger Penske's racing teams.

Rodger Ward… a decent guy and great driver

With the rare feat of having three Indianapolis 500 wins under his belt, Rodger Ward was one of the most respected and talented professional race drivers. We worked on a project for a celebrity race in Hawaii. The "celebs" would drive Ford Cobras and Pennzoil would sponsor it.

I had known Rodger since the early 1960's when he gave a talk to my automotive class at the Lincoln Chicago Boys Club, a city sponsored non-profit youth activity center, part of the Boys and Girls Clubs of Chicago. At the behest of Champion Spark Plug Company, one of his sponsors, Rodger flew his Cessna 190 into Chicago's Meigs Field and gave his talk to the kids. I had a *huge* slot car racing track (took up an entire room) donated by a model car company and put on 14 racing stars /celebrities appearances for the boys. The notables were sent by STP, Goodyear, Firestone, Pure Oil and others.

At the end of the year, The Boys Club threw a big "thank you" banquet for me complete with plaques, speeches, etc. The director of the Lincoln Chicago Boys Club, Art Weldon, had the club buy a new Ford station wagon and they towed my racecar to several Midwestern races in Illinois, Michigan, Ohio and Iowa.

Twice we took several of the boys to races to be my pit crew.

Rodger came to my house in Newport Beach, California for a couple of functions and I ran in a couple of sports car races that he managed in1997. In Newport Beach, Rodger was like a celebrity at one of our parties as he attended along with Trans Am (Trans American Racing Championship) 1969 champion George Follmer.

A former Army Air Corps fighter pilot in WWII, flying P-38's, everyone loved Rodger. In person he was Mr. Laid Back but on a racetrack he was a tiger. In the style of the early barnstorming racing daredevils he wasn't afraid to use his fists to make a point.

Here I am interviewing Mario Andretti for my TV show.

Mario Andretti and me… cruising at 178 mph in Vegas

I met Mario at a couple of races and a Ford-sponsored cocktail party. Most exciting, I had the pleasure of touring the Las Vegas Motor Speedway with him in the two-seater Indy Car when we hit 178 mph in1967.

He later appeared on my Hawaii TV show, "Ohana Road" pitching his driving school. He also owns a winery in Napa Valley.

George Hurst… patriot… hot rodder… genius

In the world of high-performance automobiles, George Hurst was another magic name. Everybody in the auto-racing world knew about Hurst shifters, (the four and five speed quick shift transmission), wildly beautiful Linda Vaughn *("Miss Hurst Golden Shifter"),* fantastically fast Hurst 442 Oldsmobile's and the complete line of Hurst speed equipment for U.S. made muscle cars.

Genial George Hurst was an ex-Navy motor mechanic with imagination. He was fast gaining East Coast hot rodder visibility. While in the service he practically invented "engine swaps"… putting hot Cadillac's in Naval Officers' Fords and Chevys. He helped create high horsepower street rods.

After 16 years in the Navy, he began working on a unique manual transmission and it was, by far, an improvement over anything the auto factories were producing. It was smoother, and in the world of drag racing *speed shifting* was paramount. Friends encouraged Hurst to manufacture and market the new "Hurst Five-Speed Shifter."

California was where hot rodding was gaining popularity. Speed shops were popping up everywhere. George got in his beat up old Ford pickup truck and made the rounds of speed shops coast-to-coast peddling his "Hurst Shifter."

Another Hurst supporter said, "George why not take this to Bunky Knudsen at General Motors?"

Predictably, George's response was, "I doubt if the president of GM is going to give hot rodder me the time of day." But he did.

Knudsen was an engineer. He respected the hot rodding innovators… the ultra-creative "shade tree mechanics" of America… for their innovative concepts. George got an audience with Semon "Bunky" Knudsen and sold him the concept of the Hurst shifters.

They were produced for Chevrolets, Pontiac's and Oldsmobiles and others. The Hurst Performance Products Company of Warminster, Pennsylvania was born and is still going strong.

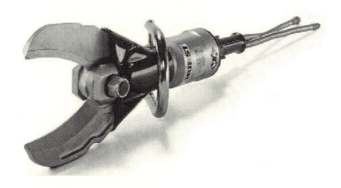

George Hurst's great invention, the Jaws of Life

Before long, George was a millionaire. He was regarded as the most flamboyant of high-performance automotive aftermarket product manufacturer that ever came down the pike. He invented race queens, race parades and built a variety of unique, award-winning exhibition hot rod showstoppers.

We palled around for a while in Newport Beach, California while he was attempting to write a book and was conjuring up more new auto products. I always admired his creativity and energy. One time in 1985 we broke some sort of speed record in his hopped-up speedboat going from Huntington Beach to Catalina Island. We went so fast the windshield broke and all the seats ripped out. George's wife number three, Lila, threatened divorce if he didn't back off. He didn't.

What is generally not known is that George Hurst invented the "Jaws of Life" that saves hundreds of people worldwide daily. George gave the" Jaws of Life" to the U.S. Department of Transportation. He made a presentation to Secretary of Transportation on the steps of the Senate Building. He said, "I owe my country… I'm giving something back."

Janet Guthrie… what goes around comes around

Though much credit goes to Lyn St. James as the most prominent, media visible, professional woman race driver, the real deal was an aerospace engineer from Massachusetts, Janet Guthrie. She was a car nut at an early age and decided early on she wanted to race. And she did… big-time. She started with British sports cars, one of which was Jaguar X K-120   and finally graduated to the big show. She ran NASCAR stock car races and Indy Car series. She did quite well with some top ten finishes and qualifying before Danica Patrick.

I attempted to get a radio interview with her at Ontario Motor Speedway in 1978 for a weekly AM radio show I was hosting on a station in Redondo Beach, California. She was driving a Chevy in a Winston Cup NASCAR event. I went to her garage area where she was on the phone with a girlfriend. She made me wait… and wait… and wait. I really got pissed. Throughout the radio interview she was caustic, condescending… a bore. Bye-bye Janet Guthrie.

Flash forward one year and I'm racing a very rare alloy bodied 1951 Jaguar X K 120 MC ("C" is for competition) at the annual August Historic auto races at Laguna Seca Raceway in Monterey, California. The car is a bullet except that it had no brakes. I started 24th and came in second... Heckuva run and I had a happy car owner in my pal millionaire developer Russell Head of Tiburon, California, a guy who had a collection of 23 classic cars.

As we were celebrating in the paddock area suddenly someone charges at me out of the blue and smothers me in her arms. It's Janet Guthrie.

"Good Lord I had a car just like that," she said. "Wow did you give that thing a ride." Go figure. A year ago she wouldn't give me the time of day... now I'm her hero.

Janet Guthrie

"The Speed King," Mickey Thompson... killed by a mad man

I'm cruising along Pacific Coast Hwy in Huntington Beach 7:00 a.m. on a beautiful March day in 1988. On the radio I learn that a well-known sports figure and his wife were murdered that morning in Bradbury Estates. This captured my attention.

"More details later," the announcer said.

At the top of the hour, more details came over the airwaves. Mickey Thompson was the name announced. Stunned, I pulled to the side of the road to try to digest the news. Mickey Thompson was one of the biggest names in motorsports and was called "The Speed King."

Bradbury Estates was a quiet, little-known, very affluent enclave of estates and farms 20 miles from Pasadena. I knew Mickey and his wife lived there. My next thought...

Mike Goodwin killed Mickey

I had known Mickey Thompson for several years, having interviewed him many times. I tried to put together a drag racing TV show with him but with Mickey it was HIS way or the highway.

His resume was impressive to say the least. He earned the title "The Speed King" as he held over 100 speed records at the Bonneville, Utah Salt Flats, prepared unique racecars for the Indy 500, built a successful auto-parts manufacturing empire. In recent years he was the maestro/creator of stadium truck racing. This form of racing was an instant spectator home run.

Mickey filled the Los Angeles Coliseum, Anaheim Stadium and similar venues in San Diego, Northern California and Arizona with 70,000 frenzied fans watching Ford versus Datsun versus Chevy versus Toyota slam banging over jumps and berms inside the stadium. *It was very profitable.*

Motorcycle race promoter Mike Goodwin, wanted to be involved with Mickey's stadium endeavors to promote similar events with motorcycles. Goodwin had a criminal record and was a bad dude with a horrific temper. With a reputation for cheating people out of their fees, Goodwin was generally disliked by the motorsports community.

Goodwin and Mickey became true enemies. Goodwin lost big money court cases to Thompson on ownership of stadium racing events and sponsorship monies.

Mickey Thompson
"The Speed King"

I was working on projects for the huge Western International Media Company, a media-buying firm headquartered in LA. I was in Newport Beach when Mike Goodwin asked me to meet with him to talk about buying a huge amount of television exposure for a planned upcoming stadium motorcycle event. It would have been a great sales commission for me. Even though I knew Goodwin's shady reputation, I went to his office in Laguna Beach. I was curious.

I arrived there, had a cup coffee and was told Mike would be with me in just a few minutes. The receptionist's phone rang. It was my boss Dennis Holt, President of Western International Media.

"Are you with Goodwin?" he asked.

"He's waving to me to come on in," I said.

"SPLIT. GET THE HELL OUT OF THERE," Dennis barked.
He is one bad guy and we want nothing to do with him."

I'm thinking, "What the hell do I do?" as Goodwin is saying hello. So I go into my tap dance mode. And it was a hell of a dance. I told Goodwin that we decided that we are too busy to really do a good job for him. I thanked him for the coffee and got out of there fast.

I knew all about his temper and insecurity and his hatred of Mickey. He had made threats to do "something" about Mickey. I just knew Goodwin was behind the double homicide. Even though two thugs on bicycles were the actual suspects accused of pulling the trigger many times.

The motorsports community pretty well knew Goodwin was capable of hiring shooters to gun down the Thompsons. It was his style and the authorities chased him all over the world.

It took 15 years but Goodwin finally was convicted of conspiracy to murder *plus* tax evasion… and put in the penitentiary. Like I said from day one: I KNEW IT WAS GOODWIN!

David Hobbs and Bob Varsha… the best announce in the business

These two television motorsports announcers and analysts are to auto racing fans what Brent Musberger and Al Michaels are to pro football television viewers. They are the best and have been since SPEED Channel started carrying Formula One Races in 1981.

In 1983, I had a deal with Allstate insurance and Yokohama Tire to produce a one-hour TV special on the Greater Los Angeles Auto Show, the first major new car auto show of the season. It would air on ESPN. I wanted to give the show an infotainment motorsports flavor and was able to line up 18 of the top racers in the country to appear on the program thus ensuring the show would not be a 60-minute new car infomercial.

Most of the racers had tie-ins with auto manufacturers: Richard Petty, Plymouth; A.J. Foyt, Ford, etc. It was in their contract to make appearances especially network television.

Hobbs and Varsha were great and did a fine job without the use of the teleprompter. The reason I have included this tidbit in my Journal is that we taped for a solid 13 hours and edited six more hours.

We got the program on the satellite for a network show late in the evening. It had to be some kind of TV first; scripted, two units shooting at the same time, make up… all in one day!

The next morning after, yes, Bob, David and I celebrated the well-received one-hour TV special. I had breakfast with my old pal Chris Economaki, dean of motorsports journalists, at the Hilton Hotel restaurant. He gave our TV special a rave review.

Chris died in November 2012.

Andy Granatelli… bigger than life

For 20 years the "face" of STP was flamboyant race car owner, promoter, company CEO, 280 pound Anthony "Andy" Granatelli of Chicago. He was an immigrant's son and north side of Chicago back alley hot-rodder. He and his brothers started a hot rod parts and tune up company called Grancor Automotive.

They displayed an old Indianapolis racer in the window of their store on north Broadway Boulevard. Many times I drove 25 miles from Oak Park to Grancor just to look at the racer and the store shelves filled with wonderful polished aluminum hi performance cylinder heads, intake manifolds and superchargers.

It was Andy who took the call from my mother years before when I entered the hot rod race at Soldier Field. Andy attempted to hire me as his marketing and PR director at STP. I declined, as I knew what a taskmaster he would be. He had one goal… win the Indy 500. He did… with Mario Andretti.

Andy parlayed his STP Company and Tune Up Masters franchised auto shop system into mega dollars as he recently sold his ocean view home in Montecito California for $25 million.

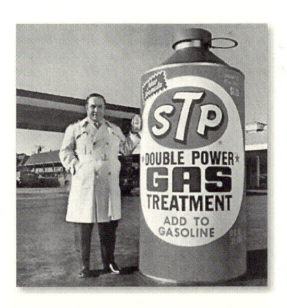

For over 50 years STP engine oil additive has been a major advertiser in the automotive aftermarket. It's a lard-like substance packaged in a bright red beer-can-sized container that is touted for making your car's engine run smoother and longer.

The product has always had a big time presence in motor racing and the company has sponsored Indianapolis 500 winning teams/cars. Nobody, not even the STP company, has ever explained what STP means.

Many gag lines have surfaced re what STP must stand for. Mario Andretti said it means Stop Teasing Polack's. I think it means Scientifically Treated Petroleum.

Andy and STP sponsored my WCIU-TV, Chicago weekly television show, "Motorsports International" and he loved to appear in his STP TV commercials. He was heavyset. He established a Granatelli video image by appearing in all the spots clad in a trench coat.

This became his trademark and he was all over the tube trench coated pitching STP. He was huge. STP was huge and Andy promoted the stuff like a carnival barker.

I was getting pretty tired of seeing the same dumb Andy trench coated TV spot on my weekly TV every week for months so I called Andy.

I asked him if he had any different TV spots and if the commercials were creating any sales for STP.

He answered, *"I don't know about STP sales but I have orders for a dozen trench coats."*

A few other thumbnails...

A.J. Foyt... *tough guy and hero*

... a three-time Indy 500 winner and a throwback to the rough and tumble "starter" days of dirt track racing. I once saw him peer out of his hotel window in Indianapolis to see a young man being beaten up by thugs in the hotel parking lot. He ran down stairs, confronted the bullies and punched their lights out.

Dan Gurney... *racing and astronomy*

... an all-American boy, competed in Formula One racing where he put a car of his own design in the winner's circle in Belgium. Dan won in stock cars, sports cars and Indy cars. He was everybody's favorite. We once talked for hours at the celestial observatory at the University of Arizona. He explained to me about where all the satellites launched were and why they are up there; for phones, TV, Department of Defense and more. He loved astronomy.

Al Unser, Sr. and Al Unser, Jr... *real winners*

... Albuquerque, New Mexico hot rodders with six Indy 500 wins between the father son team. Sr. apologized to me for breaking his leg and not making the Pikes Peak Hill climb for my client, Dodge division, Chrysler Corporation.

Shirley Muldowney... *aka "Cha Cha"*

... the three-time national NHRA drag racing champion, nicknamed "Cha Cha" Muldowney. When she hit national prominence she said, "Bill, stop calling me Cha Cha... it's sounds cheap."

Stirling Moss... *no sex before racing*

... considered to be just about the greatest race driver (next to Juan Manuel Fangio) of all-time who never won a world championship. He told me that one of his "speed secrets" was always staying in shape and no sex the night prior to a major race.

Richard Petty... *worked for his sponsors*

... seven-time NASCAR national champion and an ace at landing big time sponsors like STP. He explained to my TV audience how you must service your sponsors and work for them... not just drive the race car.

Bobby Isaac... *back woods boy*

... eighteen-time NASCAR race winner mostly in Dodge Chargers. He was formerly a backwoods moonshiner and a bit slow with the social graces. He once asked me, "What's a martini?"

Gary Bettenhausen… keep the tach in the red

… Indy car winning race driver and son of all time racing great Tony Bettenhausen of Tinley Park, Illinois whose moniker was "The Tinley Park Express." Tony was killed at the Indianapolis Motor Speedway test-driving a car for another driver. Gary was a regular on my motorsports International TV show and when I would sign off the program with my signature tag line, "Keep The Tach In The Black." Gary would lean into the mic and say, "Keep the Tach in the red… and stay ahead."

John Force… champion driver and loveable guy

… fifteen-time NHRA Funny Car champion, the most loquacious, outspoken, loveable camera hogging race driver of all time. He's built an empire with two of his daughters now winning Funny Car events (300 mph) in National Hot Rod Association competition.

Parnelli Jones

Parnelli Jones… racer and businessman

… winner at Indy, Sprint cars, midgets, Riverside Stock Cars, Baja 500 off-road races in trucks. He became a successful businessman owning 13 Firestone stores and half of a Ford dealership in Los Angeles. He showed me his great Indy car museum on the second floor of his office building in Torrance, California.

… and there are many more "hot shoes" who made motorsports one of the most colorful sports genres of all time.

CHAPTER SEVENTEEN

Aloha and "Ohana Road"… a new frontier

I was on a bit of a downer as a result of the actions of the Wall Street lawyers for *Road and Track* magazine and the Bel Air barristers for Meguiar's products who were responsible for bombing my network radio show project.

About that time my fiancé, BG, said: "Let's head for Hawaii… move to my condo in Waikiki… go surfing… have fun… maybe even get married on the beach!"

The more I thought about it the better it sounded. It wasn't a case of getting away from it all. More like getting it all, looking at new horizons and possible opportunities. Why not head out and go lie on the beach… new places, new friends, new experiences and new challenges. It was becoming an exciting idea.

So, we packed up, shipped our car and headed for the famous Ilikai (cornerstone of the "Hawaii Five-O" TV show) condo-hotel in Waikiki. New worlds were opening up.

Production work on "Ohana Road"

Mahalo, Honolulu… new ideas and opportunities

While moseying around and getting used to the new digs, I found out about a state owned video learning facility called Olelo. It wasn't a school with grades and credits but a place where people could learn about television production. And it was free.

Situated in downtown Honolulu, it consisted of a series of classrooms, TV studios; edit bays and instructors, with its main goal to train aspiring students in the world of television production. Olelo also ran three local TV stations, which televised Hawaii state and local legislature happenings 24/7. These stations gave students an outlet for their homemade productions.

I had an idea for an automotive-themed magazine format television show. I also had clips of some of my previous endeavors including a segment with Jay Leno. So I enrolled at Olelo as a neophyte television production student.

Now I had access to new format TV cameras, lights and editing equipment. I worked up a pilot script for my TV show concept and hooked up with a couple of the students to do camerawork and editing. We produced a 12-minute semi-professional mini pilot of my automotive television concept.

"Cruise Control 808" becomes "Ohana Road"

The program elements were new cars, local car people, classics and racing. I called it "Cruise Control 808." (808 is the area phone code for Oahu) We shot local activities and spruced the pilot up with car company B-roll of new cars: slick and very expensive professional footage, which I was able to obtain from Ford, GM, Toyota, and Nissan as I had great relationships with them.

My show was a bit on the amateurish side, but it was better than pitching sponsor prospects with nothing to show or no sample program. The client pitch would be based on my video production background and the pilot tape illustrating what we would produce each week.

It was time to put in motion my Windy City Adman sales credo: timing and delivery. Be at the Right place at the Right time… with the Right plan.

Hit prospects at a propitious time with a super presentation. This included clips of my proposed show with co-hosts Dale Payson and Jenn Boneza, and local comic Andy Bumatai.

Jon Rasmussen, the advertising manager of Cutter Family Auto who owned 10 dealerships in Honolulu, was like me a former big city ad agency guy. He liked the concept of "Cruise Control 808." He acknowledged that the pilot needed polish, but he wanted to take it to management.

It seems Cutter was in the market for some sort of 'feel-good' TV program for all their brands. Besides consistently running hundreds of hard sell TV spots for Ford, Chevy, Dodge, Mitsubishi, Mazda, VW, GM, Chrysler and Jeep, they figured they'd soften their ad programs with infotainment. My TV show seemed to fit their plan.

Rasmussen thought perhaps the show title should have a more local flavor. He suggested "Ohana Road." At that time I didn't know what it meant, but soon learned it meant "family road." It sounded good to me and I got a contract for 13 weeks.

Cutter negotiated a time slot with KITV, the local ABC affiliate, for 6:00 p.m. Saturday evening with a repeat the following day, Sunday at 11:00 p.m. The station ran dozens of promo spots for the show.

As Cutter was spending over one million dollars per year advertising with The Honolulu Star-Advertiser, they negotiated a trade deal to run TV spots for the newspaper and they gave us full-page four-color ads every Friday for "Ohana Road."

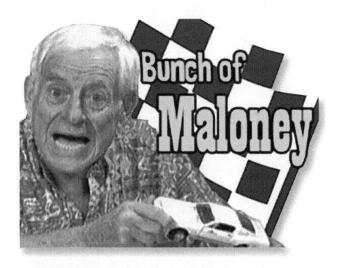

Writing "A Bunch of Maloney" *for the Honolulu Star-Advertiser*

One of the segments of "Ohana Road" was titled, "A Bunch of Maloney," an irreverent commentary on everything automotive, including movies, books and automotive atrocities, dumb cars and much more.

The Honolulu Star-Advertiser thought this would make an interesting weekly column so I wrote "A Bunch of Maloney" every week for three years.

As "Ohana Road" gained in audience popularity the demographics turned out to be exactly who we had targeted: adults 18 to 54 ... people who buy cars.

Cutter wasn't interested in all the people, just all the right ones. Prospects. We also had attracted a great many associate advertisers such as AAA, Bank of Hawaii, NAPA, Wet Okole Seat covers, AIG Insurance, Security Sound systems, Pop-a Lock, Hi Performance Parts and others.

*(Be sure and check out **"A Bunch of Maloney"** clips on page 196)*

*"Ohana Road" blossomed... and we traveled,
filmed and wrote... nationwide*

As we became a bona fide weekly major market network affiliate automotive information TV show, we were invited to the auto manufacturer's new car introductions all over the United States: New York, Seattle, Denver, Phoenix, Miami, Detroit, San Diego, San Francisco, Dallas, Atlanta, everywhere. This gave us fresh new video footage and enhanced our production values.

Another situation that added to the glitter of "Ohana Road" was covering the Long Beach Grand Prix Celebrity Race each year. This gave us free access to dozens of the top movie and television personalities who were racing Toyota's and Scions for a charitable cause.

The Ohana Road crew: John Lewis, Director of Photography, your humble author, Dale Payson, Program Host, and Andy Montague, Director

At the outset, we tied in with Meguair's popular network TV show, "Car Crazy" and this gave us neat celebrity interviews with Carroll Shelby, Don Garlits, Dan Gurney, Parnelli Jones, Billy Gibbons of ZZ Top and Mario Andretti.

We shot scenes at Jay Leno's Big Dog Garage in Burbank where my old Austin Healey LeMans was being restored. Jay was a cool guy and knew more about classic cars than anybody I've ever met.

We covered the major classic car concours d 'Elegance events such as Pebble Beach, Monterey and Newport Beach in California.

We filmed at car museums all over the country including at Blackhawk in Danville, California; Harrah in Reno, Nevada; Petersen in Beverly Hills, California; Auburn Cord Duisenberg in Auburn, Indiana; Museum of Science and Industry in Chicago, Illinois; The Ford in Dearborn, Michigan; Walter Chrysler in Auburn Hills, Michigan; GM Heritage Museum in Livonia, Michigan; Indianapolis 500 Museum in Indianapolis, Indiana; Oldsmobile Museum in Lansing, Michigan and NHRA Museum in Pomona, California.

At the Long Beach Celebrity races, we shot segments with Gene Hackman, Ted Nugent, Keanu Reeves, Lorenzo Lamas, Donny Osmond, William Shatner, Patrick Dempsey, George Lucas, Martina Navratilova, John Elway, James Brolin and Frankie Muniz. Good stuff. No cost to us, no talent fee as the celebs were racing for charity.

the 25th Annual
Telly Awards

Honoring outstanding local, regional and
cable television commercials and programs
& the finest video and film productions

Finalist 2004

Ohana Road TV
KITV4 Honolulu
Exec. Producer
Bill Maloney

And then the awards...

"Ohana Road" won two I.A.M.A. automotive journalism awards at ceremonies at Sardis in New York City in 2009. The show was nominated for a regional Emmy and won a Telly award for production values.

On a roll… then a tsunami of events

My unique weekly "Ohana Road" TV Show was on a roll as ratings climbed and awards for production values piled up. Yes, it was time consuming. We wrote and produced 24 original shows per year heading into our seventh season on television station KITV, ABC, Hawaii.

*Danny Sullivan Indianapolis 500 winner congratulates OHANA ROAD Executive/Producer Bill Maloney on his **I.A.M.A** award*

Then my TV career hit a snag… a huge snag.

I had been wearing contact lenses for about a dozen years. I particularly relied on these lenses to read my teleprompter material when taping my "Bunch of Maloney" segments for the show.

I had been seeing a new optometrist in Oahu for several months. For some unknown reason, he kept experimenting with longer wear contacts.

After yet another pair, he said, "These are the newest on the market. You can actually keep them in place for two weeks." Disaster followed.

I'll never forget the day I literally went blind. BG and I were socializing at the Waikiki Yacht Club. It was Friday evening, February 26, 2010 and there were rumblings on the newscasts about a possible bad weather front and tsunami headed for the Hawaiian Islands. I kept itching and itching my right eye.

We went home and I inundated the eye with drops. Saturday morning was panics-*ville*. I could hardly see out of my right eye.

Worry time. I called the optometrist. He didn't work on Saturday but agreed to meet me at his office. The tsunami warnings were in effect. Some streets were closed and traffic lights were turned off. Out my 38th floor condo window, with one eye, I watched over 200 boats and yachts head for the open sea to avoid being smashed by high waves while moored in the Waikiki and the Hawaii Yacht Clubs. Things were looking grim on all fronts… and I now couldn't see out of my right eye at all.

The optometrist admitted the condition of my eye was now beyond his area of expertise and immediately directed me to obtain a strong salve medication prescription. Problem was the pharmacies were closed due to the impending tsunami. Fortunately, I found Wal-Mart's prescription department was open, and I bought some tubes of salve that helped relieve the pain.

The situation was so serious that the new ophthalmologist, Dr. Ken Lin, saw me on a Sunday. He proceeded to assess the situation and scared the crap out of me by saying, "Your eye has had it… it's gone. Do you want me to extract it?" YIKES, no!

What followed was eight months of almost daily doctor visits… no driving… lots of cabs… handivans (buses for handicapped) and… *terror*.

This of course spelled the demise of the "Ohana Road" TV Show as I was now temporarily disabled.

Flash forward 18 months to now when, courtesy of the Veterans Administration, I received a prosthetic right eye. It was a perfect match and found I even was able to test and qualify for a new drivers license. Not bad for a one-eyed guy.

Now I could entertain thoughts of reviving my "Ohana Road" weekly television program but my title sponsor, Cutter Family Auto Centers had broken up their retail franchises ending with each of the two Cutter Brothers, Nick and Mark, taking over various brands. There was no large budget for my show and "Ohana Road" was an expensive production: three on-camera talent, shooting location

(Magic Island with Diamond Head in the background) shooting, make-up, wardrobe, prompter, two cameras, full crew, production truck, scripting and many hours of editing.

The power of radio revisited

So, much like my 2001 "end of career rationale" in Newport Beach when I attempted to launch "Road and Track Radio" (CBS) with Meguiar's Car Care Products, I now felt it was time again to initiate that plan: to wind down my work schedule but still keep active by producing a radio show which is much less time consuming and involves less pressure than a weekly TV show.

As it turns out, the ESPN radio station in Hawaii was switching to NBC Sports Radio in April, 2013 and was open for new programming. I approached them with a pitch for the "Ohana Road" Radio Show, a spin on my TV show. They went for it and said if I could find a title sponsor they'd slot my radio show at 11:00 a.m. Saturdays, NBC Sports Radio, 1500 am.

I talked Hawaii's largest Ford dealer, Honolulu Ford Lincoln, into becoming the title sponsor. Now, I am embarking on a whole new media adventure as I turn my automotive infotainment TV show into a fast-paced weekly radio show.

STAY TUNED... *IT AIN'T OVER YET!*

Yeah, I'm 86 but so what.

As super comic George Gobel used to say… "There's snow on the roof… but there's a fire inside."

I'm not about to sit by the pool waiting for the grim reaper to take me to that "great pit stop in the sky" and I wince when I see guys my age… even younger guys… hobbling around, playing shuffleboard or worse yet… golf.

I hate golf. Maybe when I get older I can find patience for the game. Last time I played the game was with Bill Contos owner of my favorite Chicago watering hole, Chez Paul, at a club in Winnetka, Illinois over 50 years ago.

Bill brought a leather Bota Bag full of Canadian Club, and after an exceptional tee shot one of us got a shot of joy juice from the bag.

That shows you how serious we were not about our game which on that day lasted about 12 holes.

I'm actively producing and co-hosting my "Ohana Road" weekly radio show on the Velocity Network and the new NBC Sports Network station. I'm conducting my monthly Car Lunch Bunch event at the Waikiki Yacht Club. I've also been fishing for sponsors for a proposed Celebrity Racing (for charity) TV show that I want to pitch to the Velocity Network.

And of course if you like what you read here...my winding journey through the wacky world of advertising, cars and show biz then I have another tome on the drawing board, titled, *"Pete D. Grant... Undercover Adman."* The flip side of his business card... *the one reserved for special people states P.D.G... Pretty Damn Good!*

On that note I think I see some verrry interesting activity at my condo pool. *So much to do... not enough time in the day... so much fun!*

Trending on technology

As I am sitting by the pool in sunny Honolulu, I continue to multi-task. I am tapping out some lines for my next book on my iPad; friending old school chums on Facebook and messaging kids, grandkids and even (yikes!) great grandchildren in Texas and California; emailing sponsors and potential guests for my radio show; Tweeting news on this book and surfing the net for new ideas.

Gone are the days of stopping hundreds of times at pay phones to make phone calls on the road. I've seen the change from land lines to super cell phones that do it all; Xerox copies to faxes and scans; manual Royal Typewriters to incredibly fast and sophisticated computers. So what do I do?

I embrace it! I've learned and I love it.

If only this technology had been present before this,

I could have gone even FASTER!

Life in the Fast Lane Forever!

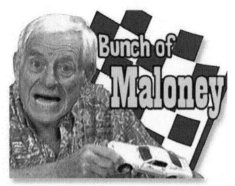

"A Bunch of Maloney" is an irreverent commentary on everything automotive, including movies, books and automotive atrocities, dumb cars and much more. I wrote this weekly column for the Honolulu Star-Advertiser every week for three years.

AMATUER AUTO RACING CAN BE ADDICTIVE

I was working for the NBC Television Network in Chicago when I decided to take in a sports car race in Wisconsin where one of my co-workers was competing with his Alfa Romeo Gulietta. I went; I watched; I was hooked. *I can do that. I can beat that guy!* The addiction started and the addictive pill was a race car. I needed a car to race so I bought a burly 1959 Austin Healey 100-6.

Car No. 1
I liked the lines and it had a tough Austin of England tractor motor.

I took lessons. I drove the Healey to races. (You don't *drive* real race cars *to* the track.) It was soon clear I needed a hotter car. The one guy who always creamed me was from New Jersey and had a Healey that he towed to races on a trailer. If you can't beat 'em... buy 'em... and I did.

Car No. 2
The car had some go-fast goodies and a real (British) racecar windscreen. That made it a racer as did the fact the numbers were painted on the doors, not masking taped on, as had been our MO until now.

This Brit sports car still wasn't fast enough even though by now it was serious boy racer time. I had to buy lots of new tools, Nomex, rain tires, eight sets of spark plugs, extra wire wheel spokes, Mintex brake pads, carburetor jets, tow car, trailer hitch, trailer license, pit board, pit tent and mechanic who came equipped with a girlfriend who had to go to all the races.

This was when the "When Harry Met Sally" mentality became my new racing philosophy. It goes like this. You are flat out going down the straightaway and a guy in a similar racecar, in your racing class, blows your doors off and you say, "I want what he has! I needed more speed so I bought the winningest Austin Healey 3000 in the U.S. — 31 straight first places in west coast races.

Car No. 3
I had it shipped to Chicago from Seattle. Now we really got serious as I went to England on a business trip and saw Donald Healey who must have thought I was Richard Petty or Mark Donohue, cause he gave me a crate of Austin Healey factory racing parts that money could not buy. Can you say, "close ratio gears!"

For you fellow wrench turners here is what it takes to make a *stock* street machine competitive for *amateur* racing:

Motor: dis-assemble, over bore 40/1000ths, bigger pistons, billet crank, special hot Isky cam, Buick lifters, bigger valves, blueprint, Zygloe, eight quart sump, no fan, electronic ignition, special harmonic dampner, three Weber carburetors, no generator that saps RPM energy, racing valve cover, Tilton clutch, lightened flywheel, scatter shield for trans, huge radiator, tricked out overdrive to give you six forward gears and an extra 1000 RPM. Then you put it on a dynomomoter hoping to get the additional 80 horsepower that you figure is what it takes to win.

That's just the motor! You must also redo the suspension, springs, shocks, locked rear end, sway bars fore and aft, special 70 spoke racing wheels, four-wheel disk brakes, quick-fill racing fuel tank with bladder... and more.

Car No. 4 was an Elva Courier,
Car No. 5 a TR Spitfire,
Car No. 6 an F-Vee,
Car No. 7 Right Hand Drive Healey 3000,
Car No. 8 Sebring Bandini / Saab,
Car No. 9 Austin Healey LeMans,
Car No. 9 a Turner 1500... etc.

And I probably forgot a couple. With all of the above, who has time for any other vices? Who has any money left for any kind of vices?

XXXX

CHRYSLER LIVES!

For a great many years Chrysler Corporation told the car-buying world that they were indeed a forward-thinking engineering company. They created new technologies and driver friendly automotive mechanical wonders. This still holds true today. Each year we travel to Chelsea, Michigan to the Chrysler proving grounds to test drive and videotape the newest offerings from Chrysler, Dodge, and Jeep.

As part of this Full-house, full-line presentation which included the new Dodge Challenger, Dodge Durango and Jeep Grand Cherokee Hybrids, the engineers rolled out some extremely viable new safety innovations which I think will turn out to be a homerun for the littlest of the Detroit Three.

BLIND SPOT MONITORING

Chrysler's Blind Spot Monitoring System aids drivers when changing lanes if being passed by another vehicle or when vehicles are positioned in the blind spot zone. Drivers are notified of a potential hazard via an illuminated icon on the side-view mirror, and if the turn signal is operated, an audible chime can act as an additional warning.

Blind Spot Monitoring, which uses dual ultra-wideband radar sensors, is active any time the vehicle is moving forward. This neat safety technology will be available on the 2009 Chrysler Town & Country and Dodge Grand caravan, the corporation's flagship family haulers. How many times have you squeezed into a tight parking space at Ala Mona Center? Ward Stadium? Costco? How many times have you backed out and almost clobbered another car coming down the path looking for a space? No visibility?

REAR CROSS PATH

I like this one! It's a Chrysler exclusive. The Rear Cross Path system warns drivers who are backing out of parking spaces of traffic moving toward their vehicles, but outside the driver's field of vision. Drivers are notified of vehicle(s) crossing behind their vehicle via an illuminated icon on the side-view mirror, and with an audible chime. Rear Cross Path operates anytime the vehicle is in reverse and is available on the Chrysler T&C and Dodge Grand Caravan.

Other interesting engineering exclusives were unveiled to the motoring press at the multi-purpose proving ground and test center 40 miles outside Detroit: Rear Seat Swivel Screen that's hooked into Chryslers SIRIUS backseat TV system and allows passengers in Chrysler family vans who are facing backward in their "Swivel n Go" seats to watch live family TV programming.

The MOPAR guys also introduced Enhanced Voice-Activated in-vehicle Communications System, which allows you to download up to 1,000 phone book entries for hands-free phone calls. This option is available on most 2009 Chrysler, Dodge, and Jeep vehicles. Also standard on many Chrysler products is tire pressure monitoring system a device I once poo poohd as a bit of gingerbread. But what do I know?

It's been proven that proper tire inflation gets better gas mileage and can save you up to 3% in fuel purchase. Do the math. 3% of a $60.00 fill up times XX fill ups per year is ??$$.

XXXX

HOW WE GOT THE (CAR) BUG

When put to the memory test most of us confirmed motorheads can usually recall some defining moment or situation… most certainly **the** car make that got us pointed in the direction of an enjoyable (and costly) period of automotive enthusiasm and involvement.

I caught the car bug one morning many moons ago as I exited the posh Drake Hotel on Chicago's Lake Michigan and discovered a boxy but stunning 1949 British MG-TC parked at the curb and being guarded by (appropriately) BeefEater costumed hotel doorman. With fold flat windshield, skinny tires, cut down doors, huge wire wheels and snug two-seat cockpit, it appeared be from another world. I was hooked.

Jay Leno says his love affair with unique automotive iron took place the day at the age of 10 he spotted a sleek 1950 Jaguar XK120 in a neighbors Scranton, Pa garage as he was touring the city on his bicycle/Honolulu's number one British MG sports car collector **Willie Williams** says his MG affliction started almost deviously as at the age of 15 in hometown Los Angeles he helped talk a neighbor into purchasing an MGTD that he really didn't need. After four months of un-loved ownership Willie talked his Dad into buying the sports car for Willie who was a few months away from drivers license age…

Done deal… now Willy has five classic MG sports cars.

Probably the finest car collection in Hawaii which includes the first Chevy Corvette to come to the islands is owned by Honolulu Attorney **Jim Sattler** who also owns one of the most valuable HO gauge train collections. We'd love to hear Jim's *"how I got hooked"* story but he's not in the habit of returning phone calls. Maybe this invitation will have an effect. Former UH football coach **June Jones** told us his first car was… heck, let's not go there.

Local car enthusiast **Paul Schwartz** says his baptism to the world of cool cars took place in 1965. He was dutifully mowing his front lawn on Stafford street when his sisters' date… a guy named Dave pulled up in a '32 Ford roadster powered by a 289 cubic inch mill.
All he had to do was goose the glasspack Smitty mufflers, offer Paul a quick trip to 7-11 and voila… another convert to the crazy car culture.

Awhile back I was coaching comic **Jonathan Winters** on sports and racing car terminology for an SCCA national convention appearance I had scheduled for his formidable entertainment talents and he started off by saying: "My first car was a Studebaker with Ferrari tires "Huh! Speaking of SCCA local Sports Car Club of America exec **Ed Hollmann** admits that the first car that turned him into a gearhead was a 1953 (that's old) Austin Healey 100-4 that be bought in

1960. His first stick shift and unique because this early four-banger sports car had a three-speed manual. Local JN Automotive automotive "sales consultant" **Dave Hallberg** tells us he got car connected via his 1952 Ford Custom Line coupe powered by a 322 cubic inch Buick v8 motor... called it a Bu-Ford. We have more *My First... getting the bug* stories coming up. Stay tuned. What's your excuse? Let us know.

XXXX

MORE MAGAZINES ABOUT CARS THAN ANY OTHER SUBJECT

I don't think anyone really knows how many monthly, weekly, magazines about cars and trucks are available on newsstands and by mail order subscription. I stopped counting at 50 titles.

I often wonder how some of these rags survive when you consider print publications are advertiser supported and with 50 plus publications to select from, the advertiser has to go with the book that most closely "hits" its core audience/buyer.

We gearheads are aware that the enthusiast side of the car world is fragmented in specific areas of interest... Racing alone has over a dozen major types, and there's collecting, restoring, maintenance, hop up, and customizing. And this carries over into the world of trucks... old, new, tomorrow's models.

There are more publications devoted to car stuff than to any other subject. Check this out at Borders... you'll see what I mean. And I say again, "How do these publications hack it?" How do they hack it monetarily? Let's look at some titles and attempt to determine who constitutes the audience, who reads these monthlies.

MOTOR TREND has a broad area of interest and is fifty years old. CAR AND DRIVER has the biggest circulation with 1.3 million copies printed and sold. ROAD & TRACK is the most highly respected, editorial-wise. AUTOWEEK is the weekly for racing enthusiasts everywhere. TRUCKIN' WORLD is for the new truck enthusiast buyer prospects. RACE CAR ENGINEERING is directed at the hot rod techies.

SPORT TRUCK is for pickup enthusiasts. DIESEL TRUCK should be getting more popular these fuelish-wise days. SUPER CHEVY is read by the Bow Tie brigade MUSTANG MONTHLY readers do not acknowledge Chevy's existence. RODDERS DIGEST is for the hard-core hop up guy or gal.

JP is aimed at Jeep people as is JEEP JUNKIE. This segment of the off-road enthusiast comes from another planet. VINTAGE TRUCK is to drug junkies as VINTAGE RACECAR is to old racer enthusiasts. 4-WHEEL DRIVE magazine... see TRUCKIN', and JEEP JUNKIE is to drug junkies as VINTAGE RACECAR is to old racer enthusiasts. 4-WHEEL DRIVE magazine... see TRUCKIN' and JEEP JUNKIE.

CRAWL is a new rag devoted to rock crawling for AWD vehicle buffs. Also new on the scene is PERFORMANCE AUTO SOUND aimed at audiophile motorists and CAR 41 RACING has something to do with NASCAR coverage.

Volkswagen owners keep up-to-date via three monthlies including ULTRA VW's. I think LUXURY EXOTIC magazine is for those of us who will never be able to afford a Bugatti Veyron but still want a vicarious goose by reading about the $million two-seater. EURO CAR is for... well... European car owners. I reckon Ed Begley Jr. and Leonardo DiCaprio read GREEN CAR JOURNAL, that is, when they're not reading HEMMINGS for recent auction prices of vintage Bentleys.

CONSUMER REPORTS is not for car enthusiasts as it is *THE* most reliable automotive publication for new car profiles and recommendations. They tell it like it is. CR takes no advertising, is beholden to no one. They don't pull punches.

XXXX

MORE HAWAII GEARHEAD STORIES

It's amazing how many Hawaii car enthusiasts responded to our Call for "My *First Car*" stories. Honolulu Attorney **Gregg Frey**: I own several "semi-classic" cars, am a fanatical gearhead all because of that fateful summer day in 1977 when after a summer of saving I acquired the car of my dreams. A 1966 Volkswagen Karman Ghia pseudo sports car became the car of my dreams. Life was good... I was hooked.

Local car buff **Rand Pelligrino** like the Big Island collector **Robert Smith** hot charmed by a 1958 British Triumph TR-3 when he spotted an ad for a '67 Lotus Elan sports car with a fractured motor and his brother helped him rebuild the Lotus four cylinder power plant. This is when Rand found out what REAL sports car handling was all about. That experience launched him into a couple of decades of ownership of true high performance sports cars including a couple Italian Ferraris but nothing turned him on like his new 2000 pound Lotus Elise with "fantastic suspension" and handling like no other sports car.

Hawaii Bar Journal publisher (is that a guide to Honolulu saloons?) **Brett Pruitt** is a dyed-in-the-wool British car nut owns Jaguars and Austin Healeys got the performance car bug from his brothers addiction to a 1969 Chevrolet SS Chevelle with a hot 396 cubic inch motor, two ominous black racing stripes and cowl injection.

After a series of after dark burnouts on deserted industrial roads, Brett and his twin brother were hooked. Next Brett found a turbocharged 1963 Chevy Corvair convertible and the beat goes on.

Hawaii SCCA member **Pete Fagan** says that after he returned from service in the Navy, he got involved with schooling on air-cooled reciprocating aircraft engines... then jets with high horsepower. His first four-wheeled acquisition was a 1963 Volkswagen Beetle. He drove it as if it was a Porsche Speedster and then in 1976, Pete stepped up to a Porsche 914. *At last a Porsche.* Then the car of his dreams came onto the scene 23 years ago as he purchased a 10 year old 1975 Porsche 911S Targa.

He's been a Porsche-file ever since.

Now comes Ohio expatriate Bryan Miller who is a Ford man. He watched his Dad build Ford flathead hot rods but when he went in 1965 to National Trails Raceway near Columbus, Ohio he saw his first 427 CI Ford Cobra in action.

When the Snake blew off a full-house Chevrolet Stingray in the races final event and then watched in awe as the owner drove it home... the Chevy was trailered. Pete said he was hooked. Five years ago he got his Cobra... a replica yes... but the nameplate says Cobra.

XXXX

GM MILESTONES

General Motors is celebrating its 100th birthday this year and I thought it might be appropriate to highlight a few of the Generals more significant.

Growth milestones since the inception of this automotive behemoth.

1908
Billy Durant who founded Buick incorporates General Motors as a holding company for that brand with more name plates to follow. Durant was a true visionary in the mold of Henry Ford, Thomas Edison, Walter Chrysler, Henry Kaiser.

1909-1910
Pontiac (Oakland Motors) and Cadillac join the company

1912
Cadillac makes the electric self starter standard on the luxury brand

1918-1919
Chevrolet comes on board along with AC Delco and Fisher Body

1924-1926
Buick intro's four-wheel brakes'. GM opens Brazil, Germany, France

1930-1934
First Caddie V16 debuts as does it's first 2-cycle diesel powered train

1936-1939
Parade of Progress ... Eight huge vans tour the U.S.Futurama at NY world's
Fair. Hydramantic transmission on Oldsmobile's. 25 million car built
1942
All car production is devoted to the war effort

1950-1952
Chevy introduces Powerglide trans. Cadillac, Olds, Buick power steering

1962-1966
Enter the Sting Ray Corvette. Front drive Olds Toronado, Camaro, Firebird

1977-1983
Here comes Mr. Goodwrench, front wheel drive. GM buys Hughes Aircraft

1990-1999
EV-1 Electric car debuts. Cadillac Northstar shines. GM buys Hummer

2002- 2007
GM is sorry it bought Daewoo in 2002 and fights imports for sales share

GENEROUS MOTORS STUFF THAT DIDN'T WORK

Chevette, Caddie V-8-6-4 motor. Olds Diesel. Chevy Vega, Cadillac
Cimarron, Buick Opel / Isuzu, Chevy Vega 2300

XXXX

The Consummate Multi-Tasker
Bill Maloney, Gearhead TV Producer

Bill Maloney has spent his working life in advertising. He started in college when he came up with the idea of a pizza delivery business to dorm rooms, fraternity and sorority houses. After college he joined the ranks of Chicago's top ad agencies where he graduated from babysitting copywriters to making sure their copy was done before they began their three-martini lunches to becoming the chief account executive for Baby Ruth, Reynolds Aluminum and many others. Throughout his advertising career in Chicago, Detroit and New York, he raced cars. Since he was the account executive for Dodge, Pontiac and Austin Healey, he believed in practicing what he preached.

A career of firsts includes his creation of the first automotive TV show, "Motorsports International" on WCIU, Chicago that was nominated for an Emmy in its first year. Not one to shy away from a good party, he started the tradition of tailgating at Northwestern University football games. This was a heavy burden on him and he took it very seriously.

He worked and partied side-by-side with the top stars of the day including Jonathan Winters and Pat McCormick while he raced cars at prominent and not-so-prominent racetracks.

A World War II veteran, he hasn't let his age slow him down. In an advertising career that has spanned six decades, he keeps on like there's no tomorrow. His latest adventure is the creation of an automotive show, "Ohana Road," which began in 2013 on NBC Sports radio, and repeated on ESPN radio.

He is executive producer, host and chief Bill's TV and advertising credits are almost too numerous to mention, but here are a few: Creator, Writer, Executive Producer, "Ohana Road" TV Show, KITV (ABC) Honolulu, twice weekly prime time, also televised on Armed Forces TV Network with 188 countries and ships-at-sea; Executive Editor, show host, The Auto Channel National Syndication,130 markets, 2 years; Host/Producer, "Motorsports Revue," WJBK-TV (CBS) Detroit, 39 weeks; Gallery writer, *Motorsports*; Host, Fox Sports Network; Producer/Host, "Motorsports International TV," Anaheim,

CA, two years; Line producer, "Motor Trend," "TV Speed Channel," "Wild About Wheels," Discovery Channel; Executive Producer,

Greater Los Angeles Auto Show TV Specials, ABC-TV Speed Channel ESPN; NBC, Account Executive, Central Division; Writer, *Motor Trend, Los Angeles Times, Sports Car, Auto Week*/Competition Press; Auto Editor, Cox Communications, *Chicago Sun-Times*; BBD&O Detroit Supervisor, Dodge Division/Chrysler High Performance; Account Executive, D'Arcy Interpublic, Chicago, seven Pontiac Advertising associations; Writer, Peterson Publications; Account Executive at Clinton E. Frank Advertising, Foote Cone & Belding with clients Curtiss Candy (Butterfinger, Baby Ruth), Kleenex, Dt. Howard Paper, Hallmark, Canadian Club, Conoco, Wurlitzer, Austin Healey and many more; Producer, over 200 TV commercials, four TV network specials, 300 TV shows about… what else… cars!

Bill currently lives and works in Honolulu. Three of his four siblings are still living and they are as busy and industrious as he is.

Everyone is cheering him on with this book as he recalls his many accomplishments (and a few mistakes), adventures, tales of hard work and determination and lots of good times.

"Ohana Road Radio" hosts Bill Maloney and Ed Kemper

ACKNOWLEDGEMENTS

Editors, Melanie and Vince Staten, Ohana Road Publishing

Assistant Editor, Kathleen Fish

Covers / Book Design, John Cooper

Consultant, Dr. James G. Stovall, Professor of Journalism,
University of Tennessee

Chicago Photography, Melanie Staten

Courtney Contos, **www.chefcontos.com**
Chicago Museum of Science & Industry
General Motors
NBC-TV
Reynolds Metals Company
Foote Cone & Belding
University of Illinois Urbana
United States Navy
Curtiss Candy Company
WCIU - TV Chicago
Hiram Walker
Road America
Northwestern University
Kansas City Royals
American Honda Motors
Dodge Division Chrysler Corporation
Long Beach Grand Prix Association
Meguiar's Auto Products
KITV - ABC Hawaii
NBC Sports Radio
Los Angeles Convention Center
Dorothy Riley Moore
Woodlawn Tap, Hyde Park, Chicago

23938162R10121

Made in the USA
Charleston, SC
06 November 2013